PICTURE *essays*

A journey through life with camera in hand

William E. Ramsey

 Standard Printing Company

The Standard of Excellence Since 1923

BOOKS
by
William E. Ramsey

The Times I've Seen: *A Familyography*

Public Relations: *What's it all about?*

BOOKS
by
William E. Ramsey
and Betty Dineen Shrier

Doorway to Freedom: *The Story of David Kaufmann: Merchant-Benefactor-Rescuer*

Silent Hills Speak: *A History of Council Bluffs, Iowa*

Final Reflections on a Gentle Shepherd: *A Memorable Year*

A Gentle Shepherd: *The Life and Times of Archbishop Daniel E. Sheehan*

PICTURE *essays*

EDITOR BRYANT OTT

PHOTO EDITOR DAVE HAMER

PROJECT DIRECTOR BETTY DINEEN SHRIER

FRONT COVER Bill Ramsey is standing in front of The Seanachie (Irish Gaelic for "The Old Storyteller"), in County Waterford, Ireland. Bill and Pat were traveling with the Bob Reilly/ Terry Flynn Tour in May 1988. Harry and Jean Dolphin were also in the tour group. Harry, Bill's photojournalism instructor at Creighton University, snapped this photo that immediately became a Ramsey family favorite. The Seanachie, a pub and restaurant that includes an outstanding craft shop, is a late 18th century thatched building.

William E. Ramsey

BACK COVER Jim and JoAnn Mortensen, longtime friends of ours, were walking away from our visit to the Smithsonian National Museum of Natural History. Pat and I were with them for a tour of our nation's capitol in November 2006. A light drizzle prompted the Mortensens to seek the shelter of a large umbrella that just happened to match their clothing and shoes.

STANDARD PRINTING COMPANY

Library of Congress Control Number: 2010912947

Designed by Phil Huse and Jay Shaw, Standard Printing Company

ISBN 978-0-615-39773-3

Printed in the United States of America

Published by

Standard Printing Company
The Standard of Excellence Since 1923

1008 North 16th Street
Omaha, Nebraska 68102

✖ ✖ ✖

To all photographers who value the priceless gift of an image to gladden the heart and flood the mind with precious memories, and always to my family.

✖ ✖ ✖

To my squad leader, Sgt. Don Hanes of Able Company First Battalion, Fifth Regiment, First Marine Division, Korean War, March 30-October 3, 1951.

Don Gene Hanes

Dallas, TX
Born August 19, 1929

US Marine Corps
Sergeant
1089839

Died of Wounds
October 12, 1951

Sergeant Hanes was a member of Company A, 1st Battalion, 5th Marines, 1st Marine Division. He was seriously wounded while fighting the enemy in Korea and died of those wounds on October 12, 1951.

THE KOREAN WAR VETERANS HONOR ROLL

Another Marine and I carried Sgt. Hanes, critically wounded in a withering firefight, back to our lines. He was evacuated to a MASH unit. He died two weeks later on a U.S. Navy hospital ship in waters off the Republic of Korea.

Acknowledgments

I enjoy this part of the book very much because it's the author's opportunity to thank the dedicated team that made this volume possible. As the acronym TEAM states…Together Everyone Achieves More.

First I thank my wife, Pat, and my children for their support to accommodate my need to preserve my ever-growing cache of favorite photographs I have taken during the past 55 years in our three homes. I admit it — I am still collecting!

I am indebted to Chris Ott, chief financial officer, Standard Printing Company, for suggesting this genre of a book. Chris and I go back more than 40 years when I worked with him as a public relations consultant at the Omaha National Bank. We also served on the board of directors at Uta Halee Girls Village for many years. In fact, I am a board member emeritus.

Chris' son, Bryant Ott, has been a major player through his editing expertise. Bryan Morhardt, director of marketing and public relations at Standard Printing Company, has provided sound business counsel throughout this process.

Two outstanding layout and design artists at Standard Printing Company, Phil Huse and Jay Shaw, used their considerable creative talents and excellent judgment to attract readers of all ages to the pages of this book.

I salute the entire Standard Printing Company team for its commitment to the project. I also recognize the Sobetski Family for its vision and perseverance in founding and sustaining the firm over the years. Ed Sobetski was a good friend, a fellow member of the Serra Club of Omaha, and a Korean War comrade.

The following friends and associates have been prime movers in bringing this project to completion. Dave Hamer, a longtime journalist colleague, is the photo editor with years of impressive credentials as a cameraman at KETV, KMTV, and WOWT. Hamer is also the past president of the National Press Photographers Association. As a member of the Omaha Press Club Hall of Fame, his counsel has reached beyond the editing of pictures and extended into ideas for layout and the book's title.

Betty Dineen Shrier, my co-author on three books and four booklets, was the project coordinator and researcher. Organizing the book was a challenge she met with enthusiasm and skill. She also provided assistance in writing copy blocks.

Father Don Doll, S.J., Creighton University professor and internationally known photographer, wrote the Foreword. His endorsement of this work encouraged me to bring to these pages the best possible tribute to creativity through the magic of still photography.

My deepest thanks to a longtime friend and fellow development executive, Paul Strawhecker, and his dedicated staff for allowing the "Book Committee" to meet at the Hilltop office of Paul J. Strawhecker, Inc. I still maintain my firm's former international headquarters at the Hilltop building in a modest office where my public relations firm has operated since the early 1980s.

A literary non-fiction work requires a dynamic closer — an Epilogue. I am proud that Tom Schmitt, publisher of *The Daily Nonpareil*, has contributed that vital piece. Schmitt and his staff have been gracious to Betty Dineen Shrier and me particularly during and after the creation of our book, "Silent Hills Speak: A History of Council Bluffs, Iowa." Thank you, Tom.

Once again I am impressed and grateful to the staff of the Creighton University Alumni and Major Gifts Department, Diane Dougherty, Annette Thomas and Connie Rothermund, for their unfailing research assistance. Thanks also to Rev. John P. Schlegel's administrative staff for their support.

I thank Karen Keehr, Nebraska State Historical Society, for her help in providing sources of photos used in the book, and Thomas J. Lynch, director, Community Programs, Marketing and Communications, for archival research and assistance. My gratitude extends to Gary R. Rosenberg, archivist, Douglas County Historical Society, for his prompt response to my request for information about the South Omaha Historic District, the Omaha City Hall in May 1965, as well as photo identification at the 1967 National Conference of Christians and Jews award given to Peter Kiewit with Dr. Sterling W. Brown present. Gwen Hershberger, longtime resident of Milford, Nebraska, graciously researched the origins of the church on the outskirts of Milford on I-80. Special thanks to the carriage driver of M.J. Carriage Service who spontaneously brought her horse to a halt at 18th and Harney streets just long enough to capture a picture. Gordon A. Crellin readily assisted in identifying the William W. Kratville photographs. And once again, Dora Joan Weis graciously helped me with her archival expertise at the Council Bluffs Public Library reference department.

Dave Evans, production supervisor, and Dan Massey, impress manager, at OfficeMax/ImPress at 6940 Dodge Street, were tireless in their willingness to assist with photographs each time I entered the building. Terry L. Koopman, owner of Photographics Imaging, a photo-imaging studio located in Hot Shops at 13th and Nicholas streets, worked miracles on several pictures that I feared were hopeless to recover. Connor O'Neill, in his senior year at Creighton University, put us at ease with his capable computer assistance as the book was in process. Tom Ryan, assistant network administrator for technical support, city of Council Bluffs/Council Bluffs Public Library, literally stood by as we sought the latest computer equipment to access websites containing the necessary author/publisher documents.

I am indebted to Karen Mavropoulos, project coordinator for South Omaha development projects at the Omaha Chamber of Commerce, for her research on artists' contributions to the area. I deeply appreciate the assistance of Nate Driml, alumni and development operations director at Creighton Prep, for his help with photographs of the new Carmen and Don Leahy Stadium at the Jesuit high school. The W. Dale Clark (Main) Library and Milton R. Abrahams Branch staff helped significantly as their reference departments' staff worked tirelessly to assist. Norma Pountney, Omaha Public Library, deserves recognition for her timely response to our request for information on the South Omaha Branch of the U.S. Postal Service.

Louise Baumann, granddaughter of J.F. Bloom, generously shared her extensive knowledge of Prospect Hill Pioneer Cemetery in my pursuit of historic information about one unique gravestone. My photo editor for this book, Dave Hamer, shared with me a photo he took of this site commemorating the lives of four young men who died as a result of an explosion. Baumann suggested I contact John E. Carter, a Florence neighbor, whose meticulous research resulted in an informative article entitled "Four Boys." Carter welcomed me to his home and gave me a copy of *The Banner*, the Douglas County Historical Society Newsletter dated December 2008, which included this article. I am indebted to him for providing me with the details of the four boys' rabbit hunting story and the tragic consequences of their untimely deaths.

My gratitude extends to the various photographers who took pictures of me during significant events over the years. Their keepsake photos enhance the pages of this book. I thank the Omaha *World-Herald* for its permission to use several of its excellent photographs, as well. I also appreciate the photographers whose pictures I selected to enhance the pages of this book. I am grateful to Curt Edic, general secretary of the Omaha Scottish Rite Masonic Center, for his information about the building. I also appreciate Mark Weekley's help in identifying an officer at the Western Historic Trails Center in 1997. Weekley is the Superintendent of the Lewis and Clark National Historic Trail.

The cover photograph, as indicated earlier, is evidence of the artistic touch of the late Harry Dolphin. He was a journalism professor and faculty adviser for the *Creightonian*, the student newspaper where I spent many apprentice hours on the "Hilltop," another name for Creighton University. It is Pat's favorite photo of her husband. As fate would have it, a picture I took of Harry and his wife, Jean, at Galway Bay on our 1988 Irish tour, is Jean's favorite photograph of the couple.

This is a book of so many unusual happenings and semi-miracles. I am indebted to all those who encouraged me to bring these photographs to a wider audience and to others who have helped in a variety of ways.

Finally, I offer my sincere appreciation in advance to those who will read and view the pictures in this book; it is my hope that you will find something inspiring to lift your spirits and fill your mind with joy. Johann Wolfgang von Goethe gave us a good road map when he wrote, *Every day look at a beautiful picture, read a beautiful poem, listen to beautiful music, and, if possible, say some reasonable thing.*

William E. Ramsey

Foreword

During the past 50 years, Bill Ramsey has captured an amazing collection of "memories" with his camera: images of saints like Mother Teresa, stars like Bob Hope, and political leaders like Bobby Kennedy in addition to scenes from his beloved Heartland. Bill took the best picture of me that anyone has ever shot — and no one is more critical than a fellow photographer!

This is just one reason I am honored to write this foreword to Bill's photo essay of the past 50 years. The photos are excellent, but what they tell us about Bill is even more important.

Bill has never made any secret of his devotion to his faith, his family, his country and community, and his alma mater, Creighton University. These shine through in every picture, regardless of the subject matter or scene.

Like all good photographers, Bill captures details that reveal the bigger story, the larger truth. He practices the old journalistic mantra to "show, don't tell." He doesn't have to tell you that he loves his wife Pat and their five children. You see it in pictures such as one of Pat with the Labrador puppies and of the children wading in the surf at San Clemente.

Congratulations to Bill on a great book and a nice walk through 50 years of a good life well lived. He has indeed "preserved his memories" and now shares his journey with all of us.

Don Doll, S.J.

Professor: Photojournalism
Creighton University
Omaha, Nebraska

Introduction

It has been said that a picture is worth a thousand words. That may be a stretch, but a good picture definitely should tell a story. This farewell book I have envisioned for the start of my eighth decade will be different from other volumes I have authored or co-authored.

First, the title — "Pictureessays" — was born not from an existing definition, but from neologism — creating new words or new meanings for established words. In my first formal book, "The Times I've Seen," I titled the book "A Familyography." A friend encouraged me to research the word. I called the Omaha Public Library reference department and asked about the word. The staff member asked me to hold the line as she did a quick check. After a minute or two she told me, "There is no such word, but there is now."

Over the decades since my first journalism position as a newsman and photographer for WOW Radio and WOW-TV, I have taken thousands of news and feature films and still photos detailing a wide range of subjects. In 1960, when I shifted to a new career as director of public relations for Duchesne College and Academy, my photography zeal intensified as I was challenged by still photography to tell my stories.

I began using this tool also in providing interesting photographs to illustrate the freelance articles I wrote. Later public relations positions at Creighton University, my alma mater, and Boys Town opened even more opportunities to facilitate my skills.

This volume has become my tribute to all who practice this art form. As I have read of pioneer still photographers like Mathew Brady, Alexander Gardner, and John Quincy Adams of the 19th century and Civil War times, I am grateful that they opened a new field for journalistic expression. Joe Rosenthal, of the Associated Press and Iwo Jima flag-raising fame, and David Douglas Duncan, a combat photographer for *Life* magazine, continued to enrich the history of photojournalism.

I am indebted to Standard Printing Company, the publisher and catalyst of this project. Chris Ott, CFO at Standard Printing Company and a longtime friend, gave life to my dream.

Out of the blue, Chris called me one day and asked if I had ever thought about doing a pictorial history type of book. At first, I thought it was a joke, that someone had told him about my ambition to do such a project. But Chris, a seasoned businessman, wasn't kidding.

The offer to design, print and market the book, along with several other companion marketing elements, was the part I had worried about arranging. "All you have to do is write brief comments about each photograph and give us permission to use your artistic and historic pictures," he told me.

In typical Old West fashion, we shook hands and the task began — to select the best photographs, to briefly describe each one, and to publish an artistic and historic "Pictureessays."

William E. Ramsey

$\mathcal{C}ontents$

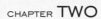

Focusing on Family

The two most important things you can give your sons and daughters are roots and wings.

— Alex Haley

HOGBACK BRIDGE
BUILT 1884

My wife and I appear as a silhouette at the famous Hogback Covered Bridge located about six miles northwest of Winterset in Madison County, Iowa. Still in its original location in a valley, Benton Jones built the bridge in 1884. The bridge, measuring 97 feet long, takes its name from the limestone ridge that forms the west end of the valley. It was one of the bridges Pat and I visited in the mid-2000s.

A traveling signature of the Ramseys over the years has been to arrange for a photograph leaning against an artistic light pole in the community we were touring. This is our choice in terms of composition and expression in one of our preferential tourism destinations — Colorado. In this shot, we were walking the charming streets of historic Georgetown. The photographer was a passerby, a young woman who kindly and carefully directed and snapped the "keeper" some 30 years ago.

Pat Ramsey and the Labrador pups. A litter of Labradors arrived at the Ramsey home in Council Bluffs in 1957.

The pups' mother, Ginger, looks on with pride at the five puppies. We have had a line of wonderful dogs over the past 54 years, including Francie Two, a Cocker-Poodle mix.

Francie One made herself at home in a second-story bedroom of our home. She fixed her gaze on a recent snowfall and the American flag as it waved in the cold winter wind.

Here is Francie Two, our first shelter dog. As a puppy, I could hold her in my hand.

A HIGH 5 DAY!

Pat Ramsey took this photo of "Snoopy" and me at a neighbor's house in Dundee. I could not resist this snow sculpture of a popular cartoon canine made from the drifts of a recent blizzard.

This photo was selected as an illustration for a national magazine on adoption. Bill and Pat Ramsey with their beautiful adopted daughter, Ellen Elizabeth. The adoption was actually several years after Ellen's birth, one of three that we had arranged through Catholic Charities.

"Not flesh of my flesh nor bone of my bone
But still miraculously my own.
Never forget for a single minute
You didn't grow under my heart but in it."
- The Answer (to an Adopted Child) **by Fleur Conklina Heulinger**

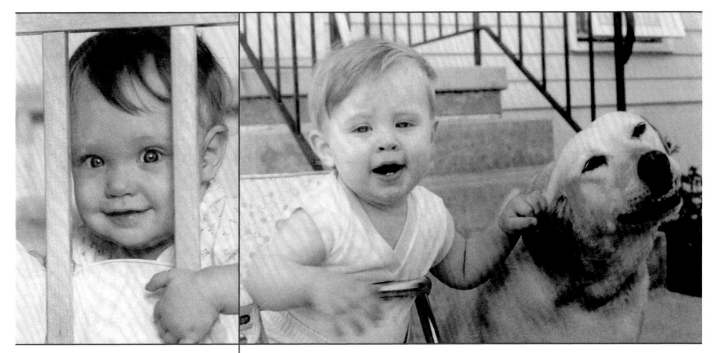

Margaret Mary "Peggy" Ramsey is seen peering out from a playpen. Her winning smile was evident from early childhood days.

Jimmy Ramsey is tugging at the ear our patient yellow Labrador, Spice. The two of them enjoyed being in the backyard patio of our house in Omaha near 50th and Arbor streets.

This photo captures a new thumb-sucking technique displayed by our daughter, Jeannie. Her index finger is cleverly hooked lightly over her small nose. That disguise fooled some people but not her parents. A large pillow was part of the clandestine activity.

This small display in the lobby of WOWT served as a touching tribute to President John F. Kennedy after his tragic assassination November 22, 1963. I observed the display and the next morning, I brought our two grade school children, Jeannie and Mark, to experience the scene. Even children were in shock.

I shot this silhouette of my son, Mark, in spring 1964 while working for Duchesne College. It was the time of year when sandlot ball attracts youngsters — and shattered windows plague homeowners — and Mark was leaning on his bat while standing in the Central Grade School playground. His target? A bank of windows at Northern Natural Gas Company's headquarters at 2223 Dodge Street in Omaha. For the record: No grade school students ever broke one of the building's windows, thanks equally to the size of the little sluggers and the friendly respect they displayed for their neighbors.

The entertainers are, from the left, Kathy Mitchell and Jeannie Ramsey. They are performing for other students at the Pat Carlson Dance Studio in Council Bluffs in the early 1960s. Shawn Daley seemed more interested in my Speed Graphic camera than in the future stars. Bob and Pat Carlson are good friends. Miss Pat, as her students call her, is still dancing and teaching after more than 50 years. Her daughter, Annie, is following in her dancing shoes.

We have a brand new nurse in the Ramsey family. Daughter Margaret Mary "Peggy" Ramsey Ehrhart received her R.N. degree at a May commencement at the University of Colorado School of Nursing. Our family was there to wish her well. She is the third generation nurse in our family. We are proud of her and her family — husband John and children Ian, Will, Jack, and Grace Ellen.

THE TIMES I'VE SEEN

A FAMILYOGRAPHY
by
WILLIAM E. RAMSEY

One of our family's favorite areas is southern California. This is a photo of our five children. From left: Ellen, Peggy, Mark, Jim, and Jeannie. They are running into the surf near Oceanside, California, in the mid-1970s. We were on a family vacation that took us to California by Amtrak and back to Nebraska via United Airlines. It was one of our most enjoyable family vacations.

This picture appeared on the front cover of my book, "The Times I've Seen: A Familyography." Published in 1997, I wanted to capture all the random thoughts and memories as a husband, father, brother, grandfather, uncle, cousin, nephew, proud citizen of the United States of America, and an American-Irishman to the core. It was my hope that this book would touch some feelings and spark some of the memories you hold dear and inspire you to share them with your families.

All in a row at Memorial Park in the 1970s. From left: Jeannie, Mark, Ellen, Jim, and Peggy. Pat and I wonder where the time went. Now they have children of their own.

My father, George F. Ramsey, was a proud, tireless worker and booster of the Chicago, Burlington, and Quincy Railroad, now the Burlington Northern Santa Fe. He began his railroad career as a water boy for the "Q," as insiders called it. He eventually became an engineer in the switching yards of the Burlington in Council Bluffs.

In the late 1930s or early 1940s, he was assigned the first diesel engine at the Burlington in Council Bluffs. He would often take me to the yard office on his day off to show me all the controls the engineers had at their fingertips. It was a thrill for a youngster who had his first electric train to see the real thing, up close.

My mother and I had opportunities to travel on the Burlington with a pass earned by my dad. He died in December 1942, at the age of 58. My mother went to work for the Union Pacific Railroad in Omaha; later, I worked there before joining the Marines in December 1948. My mother retired from the railroad.

My mother, brother, and cousin came to the Marine Corps Camp Pendleton at Oceanside, California, for my farewell party in March 1951. They wanted to see me before the seventh replacement draft sailed for Korea. It was a tough time for me since no leaves were issued prior to our shipping overseas. This was a special gift with three of my closest relatives. My father, George Ramsey, died in 1942. He was a longtime engineer on the Burlington Railroad.

From left: My brother Jack, a World War II Army Air Corps veteran; my mother, Rose Roarty Ramsey; and my first cousin Bob Wilmes, a World War II sailor and still a Navy man.

North American AT-6 "Texan" trainer planes at Randolph Field in San Antonio, Texas.

My brother, Jack, some 12 years older than I, joined the Army Air Corps prior to the war. Jobs were few and a war was looming, so he stepped up to serve. My father, mother, and I visited him in August 1940 as he trained for overseas duty that would take him to the European theater for almost 5 years. He was an air traffic controller and must have communicated with thousands of bombers and fighter planes as they flew missions over Europe. He was my hero.

He repaid that visit in 1951 when I, as a young Marine, prepared to ship overseas for the Korean War. He and my mother took the train to California to wish me farewell. In December of that year I was back in the states at Oak Knoll Naval Hospital being treated for a serious wound. When I awoke from surgery one afternoon, I saw him

standing at my bedside. This time he grabbed a "hop" from Omaha to get him to California. What a gift that visit was to me.

While attending a Marine Corps reunion in mid-August 2010 in San Antonio, a Marine friend, Jim Mortensen and his wife, JoAnn, drove Pat and me to Randolph Field, now 70 years — almost to the day — that a 10-year-old youngster said goodbye to his big brother as he headed off to war. Jack returned safely to Council Bluffs in 1945.

Recalling Special Events

Recall it as often as you wish, a happy memory never wears out.

– Libbie Fudim

Four-year-old Jimmy Ramsey waves to Johnny Carson and Don Keough in the parking lot at WOWT. They were in Omaha for a formal opening of a "Here's Johnny" restaurant chain. Keough, a good friend of Carson's, was chairman of Coca-Cola. He was also a close friend of Bob and Tupper Cunningham. Bob was interim mayor of Omaha from 1976 to 1977.

A Nebraska storm brewing prompted me to capture this unusual picture. I took the photo in the early 1970s just north of the I-80 bridge near downtown Omaha from aboard the U.S. Army Corps of Engineers boat, *The Sergeant Floyd*.

Members of the Riverfront Development Committee, the catalyst group created by Michael Yanney, were aboard. The dinner excursion was intended to allow committee members to view some of the proposed projects from the river's perspective.

We had no sooner gotten on the river before a sudden storm loomed. There was a tornado warning for the area and *The Sergeant Floyd* headed back to the dock in Omaha. As we set off for shore, I went to the top deck and shot this picture, which looks north toward Eppley Field. On a closer look, you can see an airliner approaching for landing. I made a large, mural-style photo for Mayor Gene Leahy, who had initiated the program in the late 1960s. He had it in his office when he served as president of the Riverfront Development Foundation after he left the mayor's office.

More than 25 years ago, I designed a series of ads to be used for billboard displays, posters in schools, and churches to inspire young men and women to consider a vocation to the Catholic priesthood and consecrated religious life. Since 1970, I have been a member of the Serra Club of Omaha, one of many clubs throughout the world, whose mission is to foster and encourage religious vocations. The Serra Club of Houston, Texas, used one of my ads on this billboard to gain the attention of young men and women in their community.

One of my most unusual assignments as a newsman at WOW Radio and Television was covering the Soviet Premier Nikita Khrushchev on his tour of Iowa in 1958. He visits here with the trip's Iowa host, Roswell Garst, a prominent international agricultural expert, at the Garst Farm near Coon Rapids. WOW-TV and Radio staff members included Bill Ramsey, Bill Laviolette, Harry Stutsman, Arnold Peterson, and Ray Clark, WOW-TV's first news anchor. In the photo are Mrs. Roswell Garst (in flowered dress), hostess for the visit, Premier Khrushchev, his wife, and Mr. Garst

An unplanned moment during the tour occurred when overly zealous news reporters and photographers trampled some prized corn to secure better positions for their cameras. The genial host suddenly picked up a handful of silage and fired in the direction of the corn stalk stompers. That became the "photo of the day" for this colorful event.

This photo features Dr. Maya Angelou, who was honored as the keynote speaker at the NCCJ (National Conference of Christians and Jews; now Inclusive Communities) annual awards ceremony at the Peony Park Ballroom in the 1970s.

Known as a "Global Renaissance Woman," Angelou is recognized as a poet, educator, historian, bestselling author, actress, playwright, civil rights activist, producer, and director.

From left: Brenda Council of Omaha, currently a Nebraska State Senator; Angelou; Greg Rhodes and Arlene Rhodes; Pat Ramsey. Greg Rhodes, retired and living in Denver, was an executive at U.S. West; his wife, Arlene, died in 2009.

Joe Frazier, the world heavyweight champion, met Ron Stander, contender for the title, in a highly publicized bout at Omaha's City Auditorium on May 25, 1972. The match marked the first world championship bout held in Nebraska. Thomas W. Lovgren, Stander's longtime friend, served as a boxing matchmaker and promoter. His most memorable fight was this Frazier-Stander title bout. The promotional poster (opposite page), courtesy of Lovgren, was displayed throughout the area to build interest and increase attendance at this event.

The first round generated spirited cheering for the underdog as he pressed forward against the awful arsenal of lefts and rights hurled by the champ. But the hill proved too daunting for the challenger. Stander, "The Bluffs Butcher" as Lovgren affectionately described him in his booklet of that name, had a bloody mask on his face by the fourth round. Popular Omaha *World-Herald* sports editor Wally Provost noted that, "Frazier landed 115 telling blows, 90 of them left hooks and jabs, in the 12-minute slaughter." It was obvious by the end of the round that Stander had taken his last stand.

Frazier never knocked Stander down. He was simply overwhelmed by the champion, suffering deep cuts that required 17 stitches to close. The championship battle came to a merciful end when Stander failed to answer the bell for the fifth round. Ring physician Dr. Jack Lewis of Omaha made the prudent call, preventing further carnage.

Champion boxer Joe Frazier faced the media at an Omaha Press Club news conference. The media seemed intrigued by the match, the first heavyweight boxing title fight in the city. "Smokin' Joe," who had fought a long line of bruising boxers and championship contenders, recognized that Ron Stander, the local favorite, was a hard hitter, could absorb punishment, and was game to the end.

JOE FRAZIER
WORLD HEAVYWEIGHT CHAMPION

RON STANDER
CONTENDER FOR
WORLD HEAVYWEIGHT CHAMPION

A Red, White, and Blue Tribute to America in honor of the victims of September 11, 2001. This outdoor memorial event was held at Westfair Amphitheater in Council Bluffs on October 7, 2001. Honor Guards from the Council Bluffs Fire Department were joined by the Council Bluffs Police Department and the Abraham Lincoln High School ROTC and led by the Omaha Pipes and Drums.

Among those honored was Mike Tinley, a Council Bluffs native, who died during the World Trade Center attacks.

A Red, White and Blue
Tribute to America
in Honor of the Victims
of September 11, 2001

Westfair Amphitheater

October 7, 2001

4 p.m.

Flags fill the spacious lawn at Omaha's Memorial Park on the anniversary of 9/11.

Among the sponsors of this annual event are: Woodmen of the World Life Insurance Society; Oriental Trading Company; Kinkos; Exchange Club of Omaha; Boy and Girl Scouts; St. James/Seton School; and M.O.M.S. (Ministry of Mothers Sharing).

Since 2004, Lynn Castrianno has organized this event. Her brother, Leonard, was killed in the attack while working on the 105th floor, North Tower, World Trade Center, for Cantor Fitzgerald Brokers in New York.

Bill,
Best wishes from the
crew of USS Nebraska
[signature]
CApt USN

At the highest level of the USS *Nebraska*, a few brave Nebraskans hang on amid the constant roll of the vessel to view the dramatic scene. The upper left corner of the picture carries this greeting signed by Captain Hansell: "Bill, Best wishes from the crew of USS *Nebraska*."

USS *Nebraska* (SSBN 739) Commissioning Executive Committee

Chairman:
Charles M. "Mike" Harper

Co-Chairman:
Harold W. "Andy" Andersen

Ship Sponsor:
Patricia Exon

Steering Committee Chairman:
James M. McCoy

Steering Committee:
Red Abels
Dale Andersen
Allan Beermann
Dennis A. Black
Mark Bowen
Chuck Clifford
Richard Dohrman
Gary Gates
John A. Gondring
Ivan Griswold
Thomas Guinn
Barbara Haggart
Richard Hahn
Dr. Richard W. Hammer
John Hanlon
Dennis A. Hathaway
Richard E. Holloway
Lloyd L. Johnson
Shirley Kuhle
Thomas J. Lagerstrom
Norman A. Marks
Gerald D. McDonald
Scott R. Micheels
Clint Orr
L. Greg Pallas
Bill Ramsey
Mel C. Schaefer
Jim Scheurich
Richard C. Seaman, Sr.
Gerald Sweet
Gerald M. Swift
Frank Tryon
Jesse Virant
David E. Weaver

As a member of the Steering Committee for the USS *Nebraska*, through the Greater Omaha Chamber Foundation, I was in attendance at these impressive ceremonies in July 1993. I accepted an invitation to participate with 20 other Nebraskans in a cruise of the submarine in the Atlantic Ocean off Cape Canaveral, Florida. The crew of the USS *Nebraska*, SSBN, stands atop the submarine prior to commissioning.

Photos: USN staffer

Commissioning Day of the USS *Nebraska* in Groton, Connecticut. The crew lines the deck of the 18,700-ton Trident Submarine. The vessel is 560 feet in length, longer than the Washington Monument is tall. It is the 14th of 18 Trident class submarines and is equipped to carry 24 ballistic missiles. Two "Blue and Gold" crews of 165 men each operate this nuclear powered ship.

The submarine's quietness and sophistication qualifies it as one of the most daunting peacekeepers in the United States arsenal. Naval experts consider this type of submarine as a deterrent in a class all by itself. Former U.S. Senator J. James Exon, a member of the Senate Armed Services Committee, was instrumental in securing the naming of this Trident submarine USS *Nebraska*, bringing honor to our state. His wife, Patricia Exon, officiated as the sponsor during the formal christening on August 15, 1992.

We owe a debt of gratitude to United States Senator J. James Exon of Nebraska, a member of the Senate Armed Services Committee. He was instrumental in securing the name, USS *Nebraska*, for this Trident submarine. Senator Exon's commitment to this cause brought honor to the state and has helped to preserve peace.

From left: Harold W. "Andy" Andersen, retired publisher of the Omaha *World-Herald*; Senator Exon; and Captain Bill Hansell, first Commanding Officer of the USS *Nebraska*, display a model of the submarine.

Senator Exon asked Captain Hansell, "How long is the submarine?" The captain replied as he looked out a window of the Chamber of Commerce building to view the Woodmen Tower building, "How tall is that building?" Someone said, "Thirty stories, 478 feet." Captain Hansell said, "The USS *Nebraska* is 560 feet." Everyone in the room gasped!

Although Rosenblatt Stadium will no longer exist when baseball season begins in 2011, its legacy will always remain in the hearts and minds of baseball fans throughout the nation.

This is the famous "The Road to Omaha" statue, created by sculptor John E. Lajba in 1999 and mounted at the entrance of Rosenblatt Stadium. Because it is the first thing baseball fans see, they realize its message symbolizes the teamwork and dedication needed to succeed.

ESPN's Paula Lavigne asked Lajba to explain the significance of the stadium and this "sense of place" to someone who has never been here. Lajba replied, "During that time in Omaha, our city just comes alive. There's so much joy that is happening in the city, outside the stadium, by my sculpture. Baseball is a way that families come together and really enjoy their lives and their experiences. It's really such an electric time."

Fans were delighted to learn that when Johnny Rosenblatt Stadium closes in 2010, "The Road to Omaha" would be installed at TD Ameritrade Park, the home of the College World Series beginning in 2011.

Rosenblatt Plaza
DEDICATED
JUNE 7, 1999

TO THE CITIZENS OF OMAHA AND ALL FANS WHO PASS THROUGH THIS ENTRANCE TO ENJOY THIS GRAND STADIUM

HAL DAUB, MAYOR

FRANK BROWN, CITY COUNCIL PRESIDENT
PAUL KONECK, CITY COUNCIL VICE PRESIDENT
CITY COUNCILMEMBERS
SUBBY ANZALDO, CLIFF HERD, MARC KRAFT, LORMONG LO & JAMES MONAHAN

THE ROAD TO OMAHA

Two key figures in one of the early additions to Rosenblatt Stadium are pictured here in the late 1980s. On the left, Walter Scott, Jr., head of Peter Kiewit Sons, Inc., is joined by mayor Bernie Simon, who assisted in the capital campaign to finance the expansion. In 1987, the Peter Kiewit Foundation made a $1.7 million grant to the city of Omaha for the renovation and expansion of Rosenblatt Stadium. The city hoped to keep the College World Series in Omaha through 1990 with a $3.4 million project for this purpose. Our public relations firm created the campaign theme: "Let's Go to Bat for Rosenblatt."

In 1895, the Creighton Theater opened thanks to a donation by local philanthropist, John A. Creighton. Because of a daunting recession in 1898, the theater was sold to the Orpheum Vaudeville Circuit and named the Creighton Orpheum. The theater featured two shows daily. Children's admission cost 10¢, while adults paid 50¢ for main floor seats in the evening.

With a growing demand for vaudeville, the owners decided to replace this theater with a larger building. Still standing today, the Orpheum at 409 South 16th Street was built in 1927; its opening performance was attended by close to 3,000, including the Mayor of Omaha and the Knights of Aksarben. When motion pictures gained in popularity, the Orpheum became a movie venue and offered headline musical groups. Sadly, its revenues declined and the theater closed in 1971. The Knights of Aksarben purchased the Orpheum for use as a performing arts center for the Omaha Symphony, Opera Omaha, and Ballet Omaha.

A grand reopening in 1975 with comedian Red Skelton brought the Orpheum back to life. Opera Omaha performed that year with soprano Beverly Sills in the title role of Donizetti's "Lucia de Lammermoor."

When Omaha Performing Arts Society announced plans for a $10 million renovation of the Orpheum in 2001, the theater's splendor was enhanced with improvements to the acoustics, the stage, seating, and dressing rooms. Patrons now have larger seats and enjoy the beauty of the enhanced interior.

Mutual of Omaha had enjoyed an 8-year-old sponsorship of USA Swimming when the city of Omaha played host to the 2008 Olympic Swim Trials. That relationship undoubtedly opened the door for the trials to be held here. As the city prepared to host the trials, citizens' excitement grew as a temporary pool was set up for the event inside Qwest Center Omaha. Mutual of Omaha unfurled this large image of a competing swimmer on the north side of the company's office building at 33rd and Farnam streets.

Photo: John Savage

The Omaha Press Club's grand tradition of unveiling "Faces on the Barroom Floor" now includes more than 120 of these colorful caricatures created by Jim Horan adorning the club's walls. Following a few months on display on the barroom floor, the drawings are elevated in rotation to a place of honor in the club's prestigious gallery. In September 2010, Dr. Ronald Roskens, former chancellor at the University of Nebraska-Omaha and later president of the University of Nebraska System, became the 126th "Face."

The 1975 unveiling of two of Nebraska's most famous political figures, Senator Roman Hruska, center, of Omaha, and Senator Carl Curtis, of Minden, was one of the most historic moments in the long series. The caps on the two senators' likenesses were part of the caricature, depicting them as Tweedle Dee and Tweedle Dum. They were great sports at the roast. It was my privilege as president of the club to emcee the luncheon that followed honoring them and their spouses in the club's Agnew Room. The name proved to be a temporary designation.

One other remembrance: I was wearing a GOP tie, blue with white elephants. Lloyd Kilmer, longtime Douglas County Clerk and World War II Air Force hero, had given it to me. Mrs. Curtis noticed the tie and asked if her husband could borrow it for a national television program on which he was to appear. I said, "Yes," took off the tie, and handed it to the Senator. The last time I saw that tie was a few days later when Senator Curtis spoke on national television.

This is Jim Horan's painting of Betty Abbott for the "Face on the Barroom Floor" event. Betty became a role model for many women after being elected to the Omaha City Council in 1965 and serving three terms in that position. In 1977, Abbott made an unsuccessful run for mayor of Omaha, losing to write-in candidate Al Veys. The White House appointed her to serve on the Defense Advisory Committee on Women in the Services. In addition to serving as President of the NEBRASKAland Foundation Board in 1983, she served on the Nebraska Humane Society Board as its president.

Abbott was a founding member of the Henry Doorly Zoo. She enthusiastically participated in the Omaha Press Club shows, during which her sultry style of singing always earned a standing ovation. The Omaha Press Club honored Betty Abbott's numerous achievements as it named her the 64th "Face on the Barroom Floor" on April 1, 1996.

Boys Clubs of Omaha, now Boys and Girls Clubs, never had two better pioneers and benefactors than Bill Hinckly and Edward Borchers. This photo features Borchers, executive director of Boys Clubs of Omaha, handing the "Boy of the Year" award to the proud recipient. Borchers, a longtime president of Cudahy Packing, was a Boys Club board member and civic leader extraordinaire.

SIDEY RETURNS TO C.B.

Hugh Sidey (left) looks through a copy of "Silent Hills Speak: A History of Council Bluffs, Iowa," given to him by authors Betty Dineen Shrier and Bill Ramsey (right). He wrote the prologue for the book, which chronicles the history of Council Buffs. Sidey began his career at his family's newspaper in Greenfield and is a former Council Bluffs *Daily Nonpareil* reporter who became the political and White House correspondent for *Time* magazine.

Photo and text courtesy of the Daily Nonpareil, November 20, 2002

The Rev. George Clements is pictured here after receiving the Jason Award for outstanding work with children and young adults in 1987. He became the first black pastor at Holy Angels Church on Chicago's south side. Fr. Clements became known as the founder of a national adoption program for black children. He set an unprecedented example when he adopted three children himself: Joey, Friday, and Steward.

Children's Square U.S.A. in Council Bluffs, when conferring the Jason Award, stated: "He is a father to three and a Father to thousands." Fr. Clements' care for the underprivileged became a successful model worthy of imitation and deserving of this recognition.

Four outstanding Nebraskans at an Omaha Federation of Labor prayer breakfast at Creighton in the 1970s. From the left: Sam Greenberg, co-owner of the famed Phillips Department Store in South Omaha and a dynamic community leader; Terry Moore, longtime president of the Omaha Federation of Labor and community activist; Coach Tom Osborne, legendary leader of the Nebraska Cornhuskers and founder of TeamMates, a youth mentoring organization; and Betty Nolan, longtime executive at Commercial Federal Savings and Loan and a tireless volunteer for good.

Photo: Nebraskaland Foundation

From left: Secretary of Defense Dick Cheney; Barney Oldfield, Hollywood publicist, staff member with General Eisenhower, WWII, Europe; and I. Cheney and Oldfield were honored at the 1992 NEBRASKAland Foundation Statehood Day dinner in the State Capitol. Cheney, born in Lincoln, attended Calvert Elementary School before moving to Casper, Wyoming, with his family. Following an impressive political career, Cheney became the 17th United States Secretary of Defense. He served in the post from 1989 to 1993, under President George H. W. Bush, overseeing the 1991 Operation Desert Storm. He later served as 46th Vice President of the United States from 2001 until 2009 under President George W. Bush.

Photo courtesy of Holland Center

Dick Holland and his late wife, Mary, have been strong supporters of numerous arts and humanities groups throughout the state of Nebraska. They are standing in front of Omaha's Holland Center for the Performing Arts. This world-class concert hall opened in October 2005 and is home to the Omaha Symphony Orchestra. The center, designed by architectural firm HDR, Inc., in collaboration with Polshek Partnership Architects, is known for its outstanding acoustics.

The Hollands were major donors for the Holland Center for Performing Arts. Earlier, Holland advocated for the first public-private endowment fund benefiting the Nebraska Arts Council and the humanities council. Humanities council board member Carol Gendler nominated him for the 2009 Sower Award in Humanities He accepted the honor at Joslyn Art Museum during the 14th annual Governor's Lecture in the Humanities. During the event, Gendler said, "Dick should also be honored for his commitment to sharing his intellectual curiosity with this fellow Nebraskans through the Holland Lecture series, which brings some of the stimulating and provocative thinkers to Omaha for everyone to enjoy at no charge."

Photo: Jim Hughes

Walter and Sue Scott were special guests of honor at the dedication of the Mildred Scott Wellness Center on the campus of Uta Halee Girls Village June 18, 2010. The beautiful 16,000 sq. ft. facility is named in memory of the mother of Walter Scott, Jr.

The impressive center is dedicated to providing young women admitted for treatment with a holistic environment to strengthen their minds, bodies, and spirits.

Members of the Scott family were recognized at the event, along with Jeff Wilke and his wife, co-chairmen of the capital campaign that financed the project. Walter and Sue were praised for their generosity and commitment to Uta Halee and to numerous charitable, educational, cultural, medical, and social needs in the community and throughout the region.

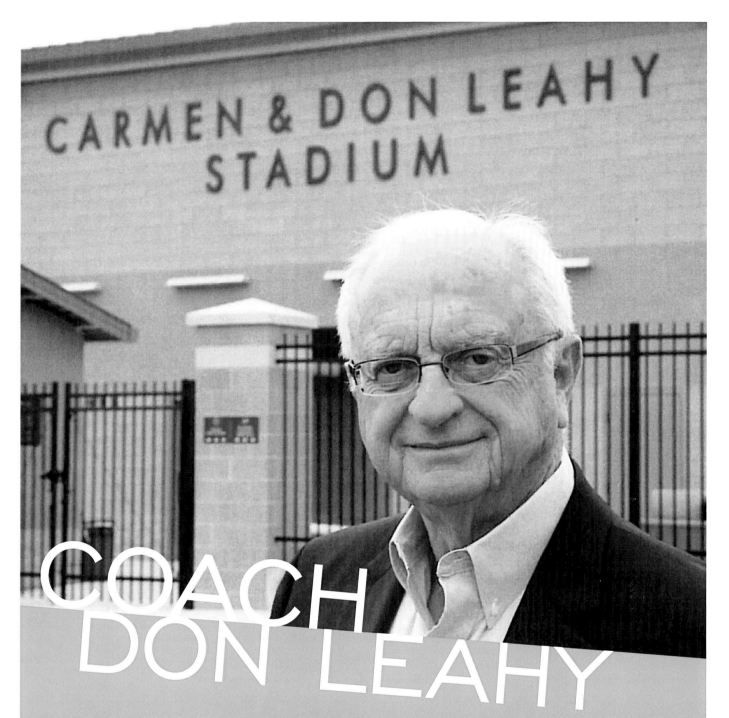

COACH DON LEAHY

Coach Don Leahy is one of the leading athletic figures in the state's history. He was a football star at Creighton Prep and Marquette University. In 1955, he became head football coach at Prep and won eight state championships. That winning tradition would lead to nine more titles under his successor, Tom Jaworski. Leahy also served 13 years at Prep as athletic director.

He would become athletic director at UNO and later at Creighton University. He has received numerous honors and is an active leader in community and athletic programs. Leahy is also a past president of Catholic Charities and became a charter member of the Archdiocesan Board of Education.

His latest recognition was the naming of the new Creighton Prep football, soccer, and lacrosse stadium: Carmen and Don Leahy Stadium. The facility seats 1,000 spectators and has a press box, concourse, concessions areas, and restrooms.

When visiting about this recent recognition, his comment to me was typical: "I am so happy that they put Carmen's name first."

J. Joseph Ricketts founded Omaha's successful TD Ameritrade, which is now considered the largest online discount brokerage in the world.

When his family was very young, Ricketts made it clear to his four children that they would be allowed to participate in the company only after age 30. He wanted them to be independently successful through their own hard work. The marching orders undoubtedly prompted Peter, Tom, Laura, and Todd Ricketts to establish successful careers early in life.

J. Peter Ricketts, the oldest, was attending the University of Chicago when the second oldest of the family, Thomas S. Ricketts, a recent high school graduate, moved in with his brother to attend the university. They lived across the street from Wrigley Field. Tom met his wife Cecelia in the Wrigley bleachers. Laura and the youngest brother, Todd, now reside in Chicago. Although Peter lives in Omaha, Tom said that the family never lost their love for the Chicago Cubs.

Tom, representing the Ricketts family, made an ownership bid for the Chicago Cubs after the Tribune Co. placed the team and Wrigley Field for sale. Major League Baseball Commissioner Bud Selig and the owners approved the sale to the family unanimously.

Photo Courtesy of Chicago Cubs

Lou Holtz, Notre Dame football coach from 1986 to 1996, speaking at Children's Square U.S.A., in Council Bluffs, Iowa. He was the honored recipient of the Jason Award, which can be seen in the background. The award event was held at the Peony Park Ballroom in the spring of 1990.

Jim and Marge Walsh Witherspoon served as official hosts to Holtz. It was Marge's letter to the coach that prompted him to accept her invitation to receive the 1990 Jason Award. Council Bluffs insurance executive, John Nelson, along with banker Tony Payne, escorted Holtz in the Redlands Group company plane that arrived at noon at Sky Harbor. Marge brought her little dog named "Lou Holtz" to meet him. He was wearing a miniature Notre Dame sweater that Marge had managed to fit on the squirming pooch. When Lou met Lou, laughter broke out.

From left: Charlie Wieser, bureau chief, United Press International; Hugh Fogarty, longtime managing editor, Omaha World-Herald; Jim Keogh, former World-Herald city editor and Time magazine senior editor; Floyd Kalber, KMTV news anchor for many years and NBC Chicago news anchor; Mark Gautier, veteran KMTV news director; colorful Gene Leahy, mayor and newsmaker; and the Rev. Carl M. Reinert, S.J., president of Creighton University and later president of the university's foundation.

Capturing Human Interest Subjects

Hope is the thing with feathers that perches in the soul.

— Emily Dickinson

The Raven Mill fire at 13th and Broadway streets in Council Bluffs became a raging inferno on April 30, 1959. This photo shows a silhouette of Chief Waldo Merrill directing his men as they attempt to gain control of the conflagration.

This is one of my favorite shots. I took this years ago at the St. James Center (now the Archbishop Sheehan Center) while shooting photography for a Catholic Charities brochure. The little girl was in a daycare center at St. James; "the Girl and her Teddy Bear" — quite a pair. This photo turned out to be the cover shot.

A future star grasps the roundball in the Duchesne Academy gymnasium, no doubt dreaming of stardom someday on a basketball court.

Mount Grant, Hawthorne, Nevada.

Cartoon by Jim Horan

In December 1948, I had enlisted in the Marine Corps and was on my first duty station at the Marine Barracks at the Naval Ammunition Depot in Hawthorne, Nevada. I telephoned my mother in Council Bluffs to ask her to sign a letter with permission to take flying lessons. Reluctantly, she granted the wishes of her 19-year-old son. "Judge Hall" and I were the only two Marine students that spring.

Handling the controls of a Taylorcraft and an Aeronca felt great. My security levels were high as I handled the controls with my instructor, Floyd Grieve, coaching right behind me. But the day he said I was going on my own, I suddenly felt inadequate to the task. I tried to raise objections about needing more time, but he was adamant. "You're ready and you'll do just fine." That was my day to solo.

Weeks later, we pushed the little Taylorcraft out of the hanger and I climbed aboard. Floyd spun the propeller a few times. It caught and the engine purred evenly. As I moved down the strip, I prayed to every saint I could think of. I was anxious and nervous as a long-tailed cat in a room full of rocking chairs. I pushed the throttle forward…the yellow and blue plane responded smoothly. It was a classic takeoff. I was on my own for the first time in a cross-country solo.

My flight path was over mountainous terrain with few identifiable landmarks. My first obstacle was to clear

Mount Grant, elevation 10,500 feet, before soaring over the mountain's top. The landing at my first stop, Minden, went well. Private aviation in 1949 did not enjoy the luxury of a radio; hand signals from the ground directed when and where to land. After the manager signed my flight log, I took off for Reno and when I was given clearance to land, I suddenly felt nervous with the number of planes and people around the terminal. Because the aircraft was a bit high, the plane dropped in, bouncing a couple of times, "crow-hopping," and I taxied up embarrassed but thankful that I had made it safely.

After assuring me the cross-country trauma of the first solo flight was quite normal, the manager signed my logbook. He warned me about power lines at the end of the runway for taking off and when I cleared that obstacle, a sense of euphoria blinded me to the necessary landmark checking. I missed a vital one and my compass heading was set in error due west rather than northwest. After 15 minutes, I checked for a landmark in vain. I continued westward at about 9,000 feet and watched the fuel gauge that seemed to be dropping even as I watched it. I began churning inside and my sweaty palms betrayed my fears. Suddenly, I strained to see what appeared to be the tallest peak. Far to the north, I spotted what I hoped was Mount Grant, the friendly giant next to Hawthorne. I prayed I was right as I swung the plane northeastward. A few minutes on that heading and it was clear — Mount Grant, straight ahead. The "E" on the fuel gage seemed to shout at me and I was once again ecstatic. I had made it.

The sign outside the building read: "Absolutely No Horses Permitted" in the Omaha National Bank. That is, there should have been such a sign. Montie Montana, a member of the Cowboy Hall of Fame in Hollywood, was promoting the Buffalo Bill Wild West Show and thought a bank appearance would be a novel idea. As I recall, we had to remove a door to get the horse inside. I was working for Holland, Dreves and Reilly Advertising and Public Relations at the time.

A second shot with Montie Montana's son, Montie Jr., taken at Aksarben Coliseum. The showmen held their Wild West show in North Platte.

Tom Palmerton, sculptor, noted artist and Friend of Children's Square U.S.A., is shown at Children's Square after installing his bronze statue, "Jason." I am holding the photograph I took of Jason as he ran happily across the grounds in the early 1980s. This image became the logo for the organization.

The photo of Jason, a 5-year-old daycare resident at Children's Square U.S.A., is quite a story. It was taken in the early 1980s to capture the spirit of the Council Bluffs youth care center, known for years as "The Christian Home." Children's Square U.S.A. hired our firm to assist the center with its centennial observance. I took this photo for a brochure, but it caught everyone's fancy and ultimately became the center's symbol. Jason is now an adult living in California.

An artist, using the photo, designed the logo. It also was molded into a bronze statuette, which is now known as the "Jason Award." Children's Square gives it periodically to persons who have overcome difficulties in their lives and have achieved high goals. Among the recipients of the award are national figures Charley Pride and Lou Holtz, and Council Bluffs and Omaha leaders such as Council Bluffs Mayor Tom Hanafan, John Nelson, Walter Scott, and Harold "Andy" Andersen. Tom Palmerton of Brownville, Nebraska, a famous artist and friend of Children's Square, created the sculpture as well as a larger-than-life statue that stands on the campus near its administration building, the Lemen Center.

You never know how some pictures will turn out.

This is a winter image of the Jason statue at Children's Square, which projects the child running across the snow covered campus. The administration building is visible in the background.

Ellen Ramsey (now Ellen Pagett), then a 4-year-old, shows her early skills in public relations. She is asking Nebraska Governor Norbert "Nobby" Tiemann for a contribution to UNICEF. I took the photo in the governor's office at the State Capitol in Lincoln. The governor was both gracious and generous.

Trick or Treat for UNICEF

This photo features two kindergarten students at Omaha's Duchesne Academy in the early 1960s. On the left is Lynn Johnson, the daughter of Dr. and Mrs. Bill Johnson. Bill and his wife Betty are friends of ours. The other youngster is Becky Stormberg, the daughter of Dr. and Mrs. Don Stormberg. Don and Rosalie are friends from our longtime parish of Saint Margaret Mary. Both couples were staunch supporters of Catholic education and of Duchesne and the Religious of the Sacred Heart. This photo appeared on the cover of a Duchesne newsletter in the 1960s.

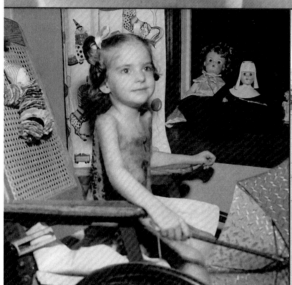

Photo: Bill Sitzmann Photography

Fifty years ago at Mercy Hospital in Council Bluffs, I met one of the most courageous persons I have ever encountered. Gwinnie Kay White. She will always be a model of courage and hope. She was severely burned in an accident, leaving scars over much of her young body. I had heard of the tragedy and asked her parents, Mr. and Mrs. Oral White, if I might have a brief interview with her.

She smiled throughout that memorable meeting and spoke of getting well. Her small room was covered with get-well wishes, toys, and artwork. Her dark eyes reflected her optimism. We prayed that she would feel better soon. I made notes and took this photograph. My article appeared in a national Catholic magazine, *Franciscan Message,* my first placement in a national magazine, January 1959. Gwinnie was determined to win her life-threatening struggle.

"On a Wing and a Prayer" is more than a battle cry. It has been an inspiration for Jerome Given and his courageous, life-saving record of mercy flights. This longtime Rotarian has constantly lived the club's motto: "Service Above Self."

He made his initial mercy flight nearly a half-century ago when he carried a young burn victim in his twin Beechcraft to a Shriner Hospital in Galveston, Texas. He absorbs all costs for such flights.

In 1986, he helped found the "Flying Fez," which is now an international organization of 1,200 private-plane owners who donate both their time and their planes. The 22 Shriner Hospitals provide no-cost orthopedic and burn care to children under 18.

Given and his wife, Jean, have been married almost 70 years. Jean is a commercial pilot and a former flight instructor who has competed in air races against men half her age — and wins! She also co-pilots for her husband occasionally on his mercy flights.

In 2010, the Rotary Club of Omaha presented Jerome the "Service Above Self" award for his extraordinary record of saving the lives of young people and adults. His name captures the man — Jerome Given never stops giving.

Alfred Ribsman was in his mid-80s when I took this photo of him on a visit to Holy Rosary Indian Mission at Pine Ridge, South Dakota. Bob Savage, an Omaha advertising executive and volunteer for the Jesuit mission, had invited me to accompany him on a trip to the mission. I wrote a story in the *World-Herald Sunday Magazine* and one for *The Catholic Digest* as a result of my journey. This is one of the pictures that appeared in the *World-Herald* feature. I enjoyed a brief visit with Ribsman and found that as a youngster he was a survivor of the Wounded Knee Massacre in 1890.

During a 2001 military tour to the Republic of Korea, our group was feted at a formal dinner at one of Seoul's finest hotels. This handsome, young Korean doorman greeted us at the entrance. He was most gracious and thanked each of us for saving his country.

Tom Wees, marketing executive with the Leo A Daly Company and a well-known actor, portrayed Pope John XXIII in a one-man play, "His Name Was John." This popular drama was held at various venues during the 1980s. Although he retired after 44 years of service, Wees is still associated with the firm.

This photo features Frank Schultz near the former Douglas Street Bridge on the Council Bluffs side of the Missouri River. Schultz spent more than 30 years running a fishery on the river that consisted of a tiny cottage, several old boats, worn nets, and a battered dock. He sold catfish, carp, and buffalo fish from the river. The I-480 Bridge replaced this structure.

This photo was taken at a reception at the Governor's Mansion in Lincoln in 1990. Ben and Diane Nelson were our gracious hosts. We had the privilege of a celebrity guest in our midst, thanks to Barney and Vada Oldfield, close friends of George Foreman, former heavyweight boxing champion. Barney, an aide to General Dwight Eisenhower's staff in World War II and longtime Hollywood publicist, had befriended "Big George" who was down on his luck. The champ later became a minister and is known now for introducing the George Foreman Grill.

Here it appears that the champ was no doubt reviewing some of his exciting prize fights with Peggy Flower (left) and Betty Abbott (right). Flower was a veteran Convention and Visitors Bureau executive, and Abbott was a prominent Omaha television personality and political leader. She served for years on the Omaha City Council and was a showstopper many times at the annual Omaha Press Club gridiron show.

I was a Bob Feller fan all the way — a fellow Iowan, World War II Navy veteran, and the fastest pitcher of his day. I took this photo of "Bullet Bob" as he warmed up at Comiskey Park, former home of the Chicago White Sox.

My mother and I had traveled to Chicago in 1945 on the Burlington Railroad with passes from my father, a Burlington engineer. I took this historic photo with my first camera, a small box camera. I had never taken a picture of a famous person, and Bob Feller was a headliner. Reaching speeds of 98 miles per hour and more, Feller's fastball thrilled the crowd and the young photographer, but not the opposing batters.

Ted Williams, the "Splendid Splinter," gave me this signed photograph. He was a Hall of Famer from his lifetime team, the Boston Red Sox.

Williams was my idol, and I wore his number 9 on my St. Francis Saints' School baseball uniform. My teammates called me "Ted."

I watched him play a doubleheader at old Comiskey Park in Chicago in the later 1940s, when his Red Sox did battle with the Chicago White Sox. It is like it was yesterday; he went 7 for 8, all singles — what a stroke!

And he was a hero for another reason: He was a Marine Corps pilot in World War II and Korea. Now there stood more than a ball player — there stood an American patriot.

Photo Courtesy of Chicago Cubs

I later became a Cubs fan, and most of my trips to Chicago included several stops at classic Wrigley Field. It is great that the Ricketts family of Omaha purchased the franchise in 2009.

PAYBACK TIME!

My wife Pat's favorite picture of me is on the cover of this book; Harry Dolphin, my Creighton University photography instructor, took the shot. It seems only right that I include in this book a picture that I took of Harry and his wife, Jean, on that same Irish tour in 1988, because this photo is Jean's favorite picture of her with her dear, late husband. The scene is on Galway Bay, a storied body of water on the west coast of Ireland, between County Galway and the Burren in County Clare.

J. Greg Smith, a man from Wyoming, has spent his communications career promoting "Nebraska — The Good Life." Actually, he created the slogan while on the staff of the Nebraska Department of Economic Development. While many slogans have come and gone, Nebraska has weathered them all; "The Good Life" remains the most inviting phrase to those who come to live here, visit friends, and see the sights.

Smith has created numerous national campaigns, including Boys Town's "Love is a Family Affair," for which he and Boys Town received the National Catholic Broadcaster Award with the highest honor of the Gabriel statuette. He also received the top award for travel promotion given by the U.S. Travel Industry.

He created the U.S. Forest Service's "Forests for US" national ad campaign featuring Charlton Heston, Lloyd Bridges, and Robert Conrad. This creation was and remains a multimedia campaign including John Denver, Charlton Heston, James Earl Jones, Peter Coyote, and Eddie Albert.

When former Nebraska Governor Frank Morrison said to Smith, "Let's build an Arch," he became the co-creator of the Great Platte River Road Archway

Monument at Kearney. Five years later, the 11-story-tall, 309-feet-long monument opened to rave reviews across the country.

David Haward Bain, author of "The Old Iron Road," following a visit to the Arch with his family, wrote, "What dominated that vast long interior was a giant movie screen up near the top of the ceiling approached by an escalator that vanished into the screen itself which depicted a wagon train headed West. It looked like a Frederick Remington painting come alive."

In his spare time, Smith carves, having started the craft at age 4 and continuing to the present. It took an estimated 240 hours to complete the equestrian delight shown above.

Smith displays five full-size and two child-size horses at his home, along with recreations of carousel animals carved by this legendary craftsman. This picture was taken in the reception area of his headquarters in Omaha, J. Greg Smith, Inc., where he works with his sons Greg M. and Jeff Smith. They live up to their mission: "Providing marketing, theming, funding, and development expertise to turn ideas into reality."

Life in the city of Omaha during the 1880s reflected the settlements and pioneer attempts to create a new life in the nearly 30-year-old city. The area surrounding 6th and Pierce streets was designated "Little Italy," where four families lived in close proximity to each other.

By 1884, the four young boys from that neighborhood often went rabbit hunting, and February 27 of that year proved to be a perfect day for adventure. They could not have known it would end in tragedy. The four set out at about 1:30 p.m., even though it was cold and windy. The hunters were 19-year-old Christopher Madsen, 16-year-old William Abney, 14-year-old Willie Mellus, and 10-year-old Johnnie Stitt.

They headed south from their neighborhood and passed the railroad tracks at the base of the steep river bluffs. They traveled further south past a fertilizer plant and a brickyard near the Missouri River. John Carter, author and researcher of the article "Four Boys," described the area in detail: "Two parcels of land, one of which was doubtless known to the boys, then presented themselves to the west, leading away from the brickyard at the Missouri River. The largest of the two, a 27-acre piece of land owned by the Laflin & Rand Powder Company, was used for the storage of explosives in six brick buildings sitting in forested land far from the local population."

That parcel of land proved to be a meeting place for tramps but it also intrigued children coming to explore the area. Some workers passed it daily to and from their jobs. The four boys arrived there approximately at 3 p.m. What happened next would remain a matter for speculation. About a half hour after their arrival, the powder house exploded, shaking homes and shattering windows. When firemen got a call from the nearby Boyd Packing House, the caller told them the location of the explosion — a half-mile south of the city limits. Today that area is the site of Lauritzen Gardens and Union Pacific's Kenefick Park.

Newton J. Smith's home, at 411 Bancroft Street, was closest to the disaster. He had been visiting with Lewis Heller and A. R. Ferguson at the time. Heller raced to the area and was the first to discover the tragic scene. Where the building stood moments earlier, there remained a three-foot indentation in the ground approximately 12 to 15 feet in size. The Douglas County Coroner, William H. Kent walked to the site after catching a ride on a train engine to the brickyard nearby. Michael O. Maul of Drexel and Maul Undertakers rode his carriage down 10th Street. Then the coroner and the undertaker took charge impaneling a coroner's jury on the spot to investigate while Michael Maul gathered body parts for transferral to his downtown office.

Subsequent testimonies revealed that at the time of the explosion the Laflin & Rand Powder Company building contained a total of 7,500 pounds of blasting powder. Speculation on the cause of the tragedy ranged from the possibility of the boys' shots had been fired too close to the building and caused loose powder on the ground to ignite. Others believed that smoldering ashes from a fire left by tramps was to blame. Due to lack of sufficient evidence, no charges were filed in the case.

The four families decided that even though two were Roman Catholic, the four boys should be buried together in a common grave. Only one of the boys, Christopher Madsen, had been positively identified 100 yards east of the explosion site. The remains of the other three boys were blown to pieces so small that identification was impossible.

When a final service attended by friends, schoolmates and neighbors on Friday, February 29, 1884, came to a sorrowful close, a funeral procession of carriages found its way northwest of town to Prospect Hill Cemetery at 3202 Parker Street. A symbolic gravestone, with shafts of various lengths representing the ages of the four boys, was placed in the cemetery; the boys' names were inscribed on the four sides of the central pedestal. Over time, the shafts have deteriorated and some toppled to the ground. However, the marker that remains continues to tell the sad ending of those young lives taken so abruptly from our midst.

A *World-Herald* stalwart wrote his last column in April 1997, when he retired to his home in Dundee. Robert McMorris had become a legend in his own time, logging more than 8,000 columns and 150 column inches of reflections, entertainment, human interest, and laughter during some 45 years as an Omaha *World-Herald* reporter and columnist.

It was my privilege to serve as master of ceremonies for the Omaha Press Club's tribute to McMorris April 1, 1997. His first column for the *World-Herald* appeared on that day in 1963.

The picture features McMorris holding a four-color poster heralding his long-awaited novel — it was still being written then — "Walk Softly." His pen name was Ross Raymond. His colleagues at the newspaper from left: Jim Clemon, former city editor; Bob Dorr, veteran reporter; Mary McGrath, longtime medical writer.

Until the retirement party, one line had been drafted for his novel: "It was a dark and stormy night." McMorris revealed two more lines at the party for those eager to get this book. "Then came the dawn; I fixed breakfast for the two of us." Sadly, he died before completing this and another book about the life of his late beloved wife, Irene.

Mike Kelly, longtime *World-Herald* reporter, picked up where McMorris left off. Kelly's sensitive and informative columns are building a new legacy for those who will follow him.

Tom Lynch

Steve Murphy

Bob Reilly

Harry Dolphin

Jean Dolphin

Jean Lynch

Delores Murphy

Pat Ramsey

Jean Reilly

A gathering of the infamous "Irish Mafia" at the "pub" of Robert T. and Jean Reilly in North Omaha. The well-known Irish advocates and devotees are recognized for their scholarly discussions — a wee bit of levity diluted ever so slightly by an occasional adult beverage.

Sadly, our ranks have faded with the deaths of Bob and Jean Reilly, Harry Dolphin, and Steve Murphy. They remain in our prayers whenever we assemble to recall their wonderful lives.

Dear Saint Patrick would be proud of them all.

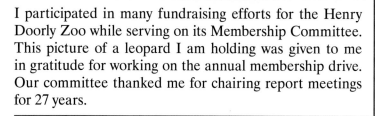

I participated in many fundraising efforts for the Henry Doorly Zoo while serving on its Membership Committee. This picture of a leopard I am holding was given to me in gratitude for working on the annual membership drive. Our committee thanked me for chairing report meetings for 27 years.

The Rev. Robert Hupp, executive director of Boys Town, presents a statuette of the famed Boys Town brothers to the amazing Lawrence Welk, premier bandleader for decades. Fr. Hupp and I were guests of Welk at a taping of his popular television program in Los Angeles.

Remembering People of Distinction

A long way from San Francisco, singing legend Tony Bennett performed a benefit concert at the Orpheum Theater for Uta Halee Girls Village. The audience responded enthusiastically to this great and genial entertainer.

"THE ROAD TO OMAHA"

THANKS FOR THE MEMORIES, BOB!

One of Bob Hope's favorite photographs of himself, was taken in the mid-1960s at the Omaha Civic Auditorium. He and film actress, Marilyn Maxwell, were doing a show in the round. I took the photo from the top row in the Civic. It was shot with an aging Pentax camera. This photo has always been one of my cherished efforts. It was first used on the invitation to the Boys Town Father Flanagan Service to Youth Award dinner in the mid-1970s. Sue Olson Mandler, a noted area artist, was commissioned to add her artistic touch to my photo for a drawing that became the invitation cover. The evening was a spirited event rated by all as a grand success.

In the summer of 1977, I had a call from Bob Hope's public relations representative. We had met in Omaha during Hope's visit to Boys Town. Ward Grant stunned me when he asked permission to use the artwork from the Father Flanagan Award Dinner for an ad honoring Hope on his 50th year in show business. In a state of shock, I happily gave my permission. In the September 14, 1977, edition of *Variety* the leading entertainment publication sported a full-page photo of Hope, my photo, and Sue's artistically enhanced version. The heading on the ad was: "Congratulations, Bob, from all of us at Hope Enterprises." It further promoted an NBC-TV two-hour special entitled, "TEXACO presents BOB HOPE'S ROAD TO HOLLYWOOD."

And finally, in 1979, King of Comedy Associates presented "Bob Hope and his Friends" on three long-playing records mastered at Columbia Recording Studios in New York. The gift was packaged in a rich brown wooden box with the photo etched into its handsome cover. Among the array of stars performing on the record: Bing Crosby, Al Jolson, Judy Garland, Pat Boone, George Burns, Ethel Merman, Dorothy Lamour, Frances Langford, Jerry Colonna, John Wayne, Lucille Ball, Dolores Hope, and President John F. Kennedy. No doubt, these three records had more twists and turns than a Hope and Crosby "Road" movie.

The Boys Town Alumni Chapter invited Mickey Rooney to serve as speaker for the chapter meeting in Chicago in the mid-1970s. The Rev. Robert Hupp, executive director at Boys Town, and I traveled to Chicago, and we stayed at the upscale Ambassador East Hotel where the meeting was being held. I took this picture when Rooney was listening to a question from a person attending the gathering.

The actor was starring in a play at the McCormick Place Theater that season and following our meeting, Rooney approached Fr. Hupp and me and invited us to be his guests at his performance that evening. We gratefully accepted and enjoyed the opening act. We were surprised during the intermission when Rooney introduced Fr. Hupp as director of Boys Town. The audience responded with an enthusiastic round of applause; they seemed to understand the fine work being done there. Undoubtedly, many had seen Mickey Rooney in the movie "Boys Town" with Spencer Tracy.

Bill Cosby is one of America's most popular, humorous, and wise entertainers. I took this picture at the Aksarben Coliseum as part of the community organization's concert series presented over the years.

"Mr. Entertainment Promoter," Don Romeo, lined up many of these stars. Romeo arranged preferred seating so we could present Cosby with an award from Children's Square U.S.A. At intermission, Romeo escorted the agency's president, Dr. Andy Ross, to Cosby's dressing room for the presentation of a handsome medallion. During his week in Omaha, Cosby visited Children's Square and ultimately sponsored a resident, a young girl, to attend a prep school back east where his daughter was a student. What a wonderful surprise and gift to this young lady and to the home.

A few years later when Cosby was entertaining at the Orpheum, a dear friend and public relations associate, Rosalee Roberts, arranged for a group from Children's Square to give Cosby the "new look" of the award he had received earlier. During intermission, our entourage gathered and gave him the Jason Award, an artistic miniature sculpture of a little boy running. The boy, Jason, had been cared for at the home, and when I took the photo for a brochure, I never dreamed it would later become a Thomas Palmerton piece of art, the "Jason Award" and the home's logo. Cosby, a showman and philosopher, was delighted and appreciative. So were we.

Maria von Trapp became a familiar name when the successful musical "The Sound of Music," written by Richard Rodgers and Oscar Hammerstein II, opened on Broadway in the fall of 1959. The plot was based on her two books published in 1956 and 1958, "The Trapp Family" and "The Trapp Family in America." This production starring Mary Martin and Theodore Bikel set box office records, as did the film in the 1960s starring Julie Andrews.

Maria von Trapp was born in Vienna, Austria-Hungary, in 1905 and was orphaned by her seventh birthday. At age 18, von Trapp graduated from the State Teachers College for Progressive Education in Vienna in 1923. She intended to be a nun when she entered a Benedictine monastery, Nonnberg Abbey, in Salzburg. She was still a candidate for the novitiate when she was asked to tutor one of seven children of Naval Commander Georg Ludwig von Trapp, whose wife had died of scarlet fever. Her plans changed when she and Georg fell in love and married in 1927. They were the parents of one son and two daughters between 1929 and 1939.

This photo records the ceremony in the mid-1970s at Boys Town, Nebraska, when Rev. Robert Hupp presented Maria von Trapp with a Certificate of Honor for the example she set for family life and education. As public relations director for Boys Town, I was at the podium as the master of ceremonies for this event.

Photo: Boys Town

JESSE OWENS

I had the privilege of meeting Olympic athlete Jesse Owens in the mid-1970s, when I presented him with an award for his service on the Boys Town board of directors. While still at Ohio State, Owens astonished spectators, athletes, and coaches when he broke three world records and tied for a fourth during a Big Ten track meet in 1935. His amazing college feats led him to enter the 1936 Olympics. In the midst of the hate-mongering by the Nazis against various minorities, the black American would earn a place in sports history with his spectacular performances in Berlin.

His tenacity and God-given skills earned him four gold medals, making him the first American to achieve that honor in the history of Olympic track and field competition. He set world records in three of his four competitive events. He participated in the 100-meter dash, the 200-meter dash, the 400-meter relay, and the broad jump

Reports circulated that Adolf Hitler, who was on hand for most of the competitions, refused to extend congratulations to the American star and his black teammates. He was angered that the American star stole international headlines.

In 1976, President Gerald Ford bestowed on Owens the Medal of Freedom, the highest award given to a civilian.

Owens established the Jesse Owens Foundation to provide support for deserving young men and women who could not otherwise pursue educational and career opportunities. His wife and daughter continued the mission of the foundation after Owens' death in 1981.

The Jason Award is given to those who have demonstrated an extraordinary degree of contribution and commitment to children or whose personal lives exemplify the vision, courage, and will needed to embrace the challenges of life.

The 1997 Jason Award recipients included: National honoree, Dr. Tom Osborne, head football coach at the University of Nebraska; Council Bluffs recipient, John Allen, Hy-Vee Grocery executive; and Omaha honorees, Mike and Gail Yanney. Mike was president of America First Companies.

A photo of some dear friends at a Saint Margaret Mary Founders Day Dinner in 1987. Tal Anderson (left), owner of Baxter Chrysler Jeep Dodge automotive company for many years, was a prominent businessman and Catholic Church leader. Tal died in August 2009. Monsignor Peter F. Dunne (center), longtime pastor of Saint Margaret Mary Church, was assigned to Boys Town in his early priesthood days. Mary Joy Anderson (right), Tal's widow. I believe it was also a birthday celebration for Monsignor Dunne — no age listed!

The late and beloved Rev. Carl Reinert, S.J., longtime Creighton University president and community leader, is in attractive company in this photo. I took this picture in the mid-1960s following the annual Creighton University Alpha Sigma Nu lecture, given by the legendary actress Loretta Young. Young is flanked by Jean Reilly on the left and my wife, Pat Ramsey, on the right. It was a fine lecture, as I recall, and Young lived up to her image as a beautiful and friendly movie star.

Nebraska's Ted Kooser, U.S. Poet Laureate Consultant in Poetry from 2004 to 2006, received the Sower recognition from the NEBRASKAland Foundation Awards in 2006 at the State Capitol Building in Lincoln. The NEBRASKAland Foundation strives to enrich the value of Nebraska's Good Life for our citizens from all walks of life and to portray and promote the quality of this life to our visitors and residents.

Kooser's prose and poetry reflect the work ethic and values of individuals and families whose roots have been firmly planted in the Great Plains for generations. A Visiting Professor at the University of Nebraska-Lincoln, Kooser has written 12 collections of poetry. He received the 2005 Pulitzer Prize for Poetry for his book, "Delights and Shadows," published by Copper Canyon Press in 2004. He currently hosts the weekly newspaper project "American Life in Poetry."

One of the charitable organizations closest to my heart is The Salvation Army. I have been on the Advisory Board for years, and our firm served as public relations counsel for some years. It was my privilege to head the Tree of Lights campaign twice along with community leader and auto dealer, Roy Smith, who died in September 2010.

I am pictured with one of the Army's most generous benefactors, Christina Hixson. Hixson is the sole trustee of the Lied Foundation Trust, established in 1972 by Ernst F. Lied to honor his parents, Ernst M. and Ida K. Lied. We are standing in front of the Army's huge human services center in Omaha the day the facility became the Lied Renaissance Center in May 1990. The facility, located at 3612 Cuming Street, had been Methodist Hospital.

Nebraska Methodist Health System transferred the 5-acre midtown location to The Salvation Army as a gift. It became the largest donation ever presented to the Army in Omaha; included were buildings, furnishings, and all non-medical equipment. The value exceeded $2 million.

The Lied Renaissance Center is considered the flagship of the Army's Western Division; it is recognized as the world's largest social services agency under one roof, offering more than 24 programs from child daycare to services for older citizens.

Photo: Salvation Army Staffer

Two of my sports heroes in this area are from left: John "Red" McManus, longtime Creighton University basketball coach, and Jack Payne, WOW Radio/TV Sports Director, standing in front of the Omaha Civic Auditorium.

Payne was my first boss when I was hired by WOW and WOW-TV after graduating from Creighton University in 1955. Jim McGaffin, news director at the radio and TV stations, hired me and assigned me to be Payne's assistant. It was a dream come true for an avid sports fan and participant. He broadcast University of Nebraska football and Creighton University basketball among his many other assignments, including serving as the voice of the College World Series for many years. Payne was a role model as I began my journalistic journey.

"Red" McManus was a fiery and dedicated coach in his many years at the helm of the Bluejays basketball teams. Both Payne and McManus had been outstanding high school and college athletes. McManus had the fire of coach Bobby Knight and the gentlemanly class of coach John Wooden.

A historic figure and gifted photojournalist, Rudy Smith is also a dedicated community volunteer and my good friend. He has lived life to the fullest from roots that challenged his very being. Smith is standing at the site of former Omaha *World-Herald* building, at 14th and Dodge Streets.

Smith graduated from the University of Nebraska-Omaha and is one of the early black journalists to have that distinction. After an assortment of jobs, he turned to the Omaha *World-Herald* for an opportunity to pursue his dream of being a writer and photographer. After many twists and turns on his chosen career path, Smith emerged as a leading photographer for the newspaper for many years. His eye for the unusual, blended with his creative skills, resulted in awards and recognition from his colleagues and the newspaper's readers. He was a pioneer in his newspaper experience and is proud of his many achievements. The Omaha Press Club inducted him into its Hall of Fame in 2010.

His recent retirement has opened new doors for Smith, particularly for increasing his volunteer commitment for his church and various youth care organizations.

Dr. Lee G. Simmons and his wife Marie are holding a baby gorilla from the Henry Doorly Zoo, where Dr. Simmons served as its director for 39 years. During those years, Marie would frequently care for at-risk newborn animals at their home.

They came to Omaha in December 1966, when Dr. Simmons became a staff veterinarian at the zoo; soon he became an assistant director, and in 1970 he was appointed director. During his very active career, "Doc" has traveled and worked in 36 countries, including Antarctica. He is a sought-after consultant on wildlife and has received numerous awards and honors for his dedicated work with zoo animals.

Dr. Simmons brought unprecedented growth to the Henry Doorly Zoo during his time there, including a dramatic increase in zoo attendance. It ranks as Nebraska's top attraction, with more than 25 million visitors during the past 40 years. The zoo added many major exhibits under his leadership, including the Lied Jungle, Desert Dome, Kingdoms of the Night, Scott Aquarium, Cat Complex, Hubbard Gorilla Valley, and the Hubbard Orangutan Forest.

Since opening in 1894 as the Riverview Park Zoo, the Henry Doorly Zoo has expanded to 130 acres and became nationally renowned for its leadership in animal conservation and research. Its mission is conservation, research, recreation, and education.

Gene Skinner was my first employee at Bill Ramsey Associates, Inc., and also one of my role models and a good friend. He was a historic figure who became the first African American to hold the positions of principal, director, and assistant superintendent in the Omaha Public Schools system.

In 1981 when my wife, Pat, and I opened our door for business, Skinner was one of the first people to call us. He told me that he was looking for a job. I was shocked and told him that I was just getting started and had only one client. He told me he could help and he didn't want to be paid! Being a smart businessman, I knew that was a deal I could not ignore.

Omaha National Bank executive Mike Yanney had offered me two offices while I looked for my firm's first official address. Skinner and I each had a fine office and began what has now become a 30-year-old advertising and public relations firm.

A few new clients later, we moved to 4913 Dodge Street. This address was home to the Hilltop House for years, one of the area's premier restaurants.

In 1996, Skinner Magnet Center opened at 4304 North 33rd Street. The school is home to students in kindergarten through 6th grade and emphasizes math, technology, and the performing arts. Gene always encouraged his students to do their best and rewarded their efforts with pep talks and kind words. He is gone now but his legacy in education lives on.

Supreme Court Judge Clarence Thomas is seen at the Omaha Press Club in the 1990s. He had addressed an Omaha Bar Association assembly and paused to visit with the club's chef, Don Lewis. I had been taking photos when the chef told me as we looked through the window into the private dining room, "I really admire Judge Thomas." I told him that I would take a photo of him with the judge. He was reluctant to accept the offer until I convinced him that it would be alright. I went into the dining room and told Justice Thomas about my friend, to which he replied, "I would be happy to have the picture taken with Don. I always stay close to the chefs." They had a good visit and I sent photos to both Judge Thomas and Lewis.

The Western Historic Trails Center in Council Bluffs was dedicated October 4, 1997. Our public relations firm was asked to handle the grand opening — a three-day celebration of Council Bluffs history and a tribute to the courage and persistence of the pioneers, the gold rush masses, and those travelers fleeing religious persecution.

Community leaders were honored at a formal dinner where they were recognized for their efforts to create this historical site, which serves as a tribute to the brave men, women, and children who risked their lives carrying this young nation's development west toward the Pacific. The speaker at this dinner was Dr. Stephen Ambrose, renowned historian and author of compelling books. That evening he spoke about his bestselling book "Undaunted Courage," which recounts the Lewis and Clark Expedition.

From left, I stand next to Dr. Ambrose, along with Ted Hillmer, Regional Chief of Maintenance U.S. Park Service, as we toured the building.

Photo: Ramsey Public Relations staff

Front row from left: Vince Finocchiaro, Larry McGinley, Dr. Patrick Brookhouser, Harry Koch, and Lloyd "Buzz" Mattson
Back row from left: Bill Gorman, Tom Nash, Tom Burke, David "Big Al" Goldstein, Dr. Howard Dooley, Cella Quinn, Jim Suttle, Judge Lyle Strom, Bill Ramsey, Steve McCollister, Ken Kampfe, and Mal Hansen

This photo, taken in June 1999 by a fellow Rotarian, features a gathering of past presidents of the Rotary Club of Omaha (Downtown Rotary).

Omaha's Rotary Club will celebrate its centennial in 2011. "Service above self" is our cherished motto and service to humankind has always been our mission.

I asked an obliging studio technician to take this photograph of Roger Welsch and me following the taping of the popular Nebraska ETV weekly series, "Roger Welsch &," on September 25, 1998. Roger invited me to be interviewed following the publication of my second book, "The Times I've Seen: A Familyography." When he asked about the content, I told him it was a series of vignettes and essays and photographs featuring times that have entertained me, frightened me, inspired me, and certainly shaped my life.

It was quite an honor to appear on the "Roger Welsch &" program. This state folklorist, author, and humorist is an excellent interviewer and I enjoyed the experience. Many will also remember Welsch from his appearances on the CBS News Sunday Morning program when he was featured in a segment entitled "Postcards from Nebraska." He lives in Dannebrog, Nebraska, and became the 2005 winner of the Henry Fonda Award presented by the State of Nebraska Travel and Tourism Division.

Harry A. Trustin was a civil engineer and a political and civic leader. In 1899, he arrived in Omaha from Chicago at age five; by the time he was six, Harry sold newspapers at the corner of 17th and Farnam to help support his parents and his six sisters. He worked as a draftsman for the Union Pacific Railroad. The company sent him to Armour Tech Engineering School in Chicago for one semester. To cover his expenses, he engaged in boxing at the YMCA for $25 per fight and remained undefeated. Trustin served in the 318th Engineering Company in World War I and was severely wounded before the armistice was signed. He was honored with a Purple Heart and a battlefield commission of 2nd Lieutenant.

In the years that followed, Trustin married his sweetheart, Bess Adler, and established a building materials company presently called Porter-Trustin-Carlson. Leading organizations in the city formed the Independent Voter League and Trustin was selected by the American Legion to be a candidate for the position of City Commissioner (forerunner of Omaha's City Council). That election launched Trustin's 40-year public service career in Omaha where, over the years, he was honored by numerous organizations for his dedication and service. He died in 1979.

On June 4, 2009, the city held a street naming ceremony in appreciation of this man's service to the community. A new sign was unveiled, identifying the street: Harry A. Trustin Riverfront Drive. Grateful family, friends, and political and civic representatives applauded this man and recognized and remembered with gratitude his lifetime achievements.

Artist: Gorden Bennett, 1933
Courtesy: Trustin Family

"Fertile Ground," a mural created by internationally acclaimed Philadelphia artist Meg Saligman, is the largest public art project in Omaha's history. The mural measures an incredible 32,509 square feet. Ranked as one of the largest outdoor murals in the country, "Fertile Ground" tells the story of Omaha's past, present, and future through the colorful and inviting images portrayed.

The mural was completed in June 2009. It is located on the east and north walls of the Energy Systems building at 13th and Webster streets. The city's citizens and visitors alike are indebted to the Peter Kiewit Foundation for initiating and funding the project in 2006. Lyn Wallin Ziegenbein, Peter Kiewit Foundation executive director, said, "Peter Kiewit loved his hometown and he was especially committed to the vitality of downtown. We can think of no better place to present a project of this magnitude as a tribute to our community and citizens than in the heart of downtown Omaha."

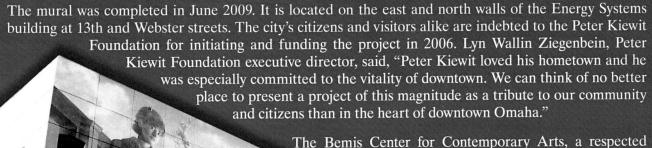

The Bemis Center for Contemporary Arts, a respected leader in public art programs, managed the planning and all aspects for the maintenance and coordination of the completed mural.

It was given as a gift to the people of Nebraska and the city of Omaha.

A historic family from Wolfville, Nova Scotia, Canada, poses in front of The Dodge House in Council Bluffs, a National Historic Landmark, in June 2009. From left: Dr. Paul Kinsman, great nephew of Colonel William H. Kinsman; his wife, Sharon Kinsman; and their son, Benjamin Kinsman, great-great nephew of the Civil War hero. With the help of General Grenville M. Dodge, Kinsman's remains were recovered in 1902 from Black River Bayou, Mississippi, where he was killed in battle May 17, 1863. Col. Kinsman had previously pursued simultaneous careers in teaching, law, and journalism at the *Daily Nonpareil* in Council Bluffs before responding to the call of duty during the Civil War.

The Kinsman Monument is located at 308 LaFayette Avenue, at Fairview Cemetery in Council Bluffs. This Civil War memorial was built to honor Colonel William H. Kinsman and veterans of the Civil War. The text on the base of the monument describes the battle, Kinsman's fatal wound, and his death. He was buried at the site of the battle. With the help of General Grenville M. Dodge, Kinsman's remains were recovered and returned to Council Bluffs on May 17, 1902, where veterans of Kinsman's command gathered to celebrate his life, military career, and devotion to the Union.

A likeness of Colonel William H. Kinsman appears on the monument, which is surrounded by actual Civil War cannons.

Plaque on the Grenville M. Dodge family mausoleum at Walnut Hill Cemetery

On January 16, 1988, Margre Durham announced the Henningson Memorial Campanile & Henningson Plaza at the University of Nebraska-Omaha as a gift to honor the memory of her father, mother, and sister. The tower stands 168 feet tall and a carillon of 47 bells from France toll the hours, greet and congratulate students, provide enriching concerts for special events, and commencement ceremonies. A handsome plaza surrounding the campanile has created a favorite landmark in the center of the school's main campus.

The memorial was dedicated on May 18, 1989, in ceremonies surrounding the campanile and its plaza-garden site. Honoring her parents, Henning H. Henningson and Rose P. Henningson, and sister, Helen Henningson Grimes, Margre said, "This campanile is a reflection of my parents' and sister's loyalty to this community in so many ways. My sister attended the Municipal University of Omaha; my mother loved music, and my father, although he was born in Iowa, was proud of living in Omaha."

Margre Durham died in 1999, and on July 4, 2005, a charming plaque was placed inside the campanile to honor her life. The inscription reads:

A lifetime dedicated to the betterment of the community through education, Margre H. Durham exemplified the finest qualities of leadership and spirit. July 4, 2005

Charles W. "Chuck" Durham, Margre's husband, died April 5, 2008, leaving an unmatched legacy to the University of Nebraska-Omaha, the University of Nebraska Medical Center, and to the city of Omaha.

HENNINGSON CAMPANILE

MARGRE HENNINGSON DURHAM

A LIFETIME DEDICATED TO THE
BETTERMENT OF THE COMMUNITY
THROUGH EDUCATION, MARGRE H. DURHAM
EXEMPLIFIED THE FINEST
QUALITIES OF LEADERSHIP AND SPIRIT.

JULY 4, 2005

Boys Town
Father Flanagan Award
for Service to Youth

Courtesy of Boys Town Hall of History

In 1951, Mildred F. Jefferson became the first black woman graduate of Harvard Medical School. A three-term president of the National Right to Life Committee, Dr. Jefferson was a leader and one of the most eloquent spokespersons for the Pro Life forces seeking a Constitutional Amendment prohibiting abortion.

Dr. Jefferson was a longtime practicing general surgeon and assistant clinical professor at Boston University Medical Center. She was the fourth person chosen to receive the Father Edward Flanagan Service to Youth Award in 1978.

From left: Victor Welles, mayor of Boys Town; Dr. Jefferson, honoree; Rev. Robert Hupp, director, Boys Town

1978
The Father Flanagan Award
for Service to Youth
Presented to

Dr. Mildred F. Jefferson

For the healing skills she practices and teaches to a new generation of medical practitioners at Boston University . . .

For the pride and hope of a people aroused by her distinguished career and as the first black woman to graduate from the Harvard Medical School . . .

For her eloquent and self-sacrificing labors in behalf of the unborn as three-term President of the National Right to Life Committee . . .

For her faithfulness to the cause of service to youth — even to the unborn — a faith and cause shared by Father Flanagan, in whose grateful memory this award is given.

June 15, 1978

(Rev.) Robert P. Hupp
Director
Father Flanagan's Boys' Home
Boys Town, Nebraska

The Most Reverend Daniel E. Sheehan
Archbishop of Omaha
President, Board of Directors, Boys Town

I took this portrait of the Rev. George Maloney, S.J., at Duchesne College and Academy in the 1960s. Fr. Maloney, a faculty member at Fordham University in New York, was conducting a retreat at the college. I had the privilege of assisting him during his visit to Duchesne.

Those who still miss the grand architecture that added a stately beauty to our downtown area fondly recall the "Old Post Office" building located at 16th and Dodge streets in Omaha. O.J. King was the engineer for the project and John Latenser, Sr., served as architect. He used the Richardson Romanesque style for the structure and St. Cloud pink granite for the basement and first story. The next three floors were made of sandstone. The five entrances featured polished granite columns that supported stone archways; the main entrance faced 16th Street on the east side of the building. The building was capped with a 190-foot clock tower that had clocks on all four sides. The center of the atrium court featured a 100-foot-square skylight and copper roofing on the remaining areas.

Completed in 1906, this architectural treasure was destined for destruction when in the early 1960s the General Services Administration of the Federal Government decided it was too costly to maintain. Others had previously expressed their displeasure by saying it was not fit for an expanding metropolitan city. Although numerous plans to redevelop this landmark were submitted none materialized, and in 1966 the building was demolished.

Admiring Architecture

We shape our buildings; thereafter they shape us.

— Winston Churchill

Architect Leo A Daly designed One First National Center, located at 1601 Dodge Street. With 45 floors above ground, it is the tallest building in Nebraska and the tallest structure between Minneapolis and Denver. Designers incorporated the ornamental terra cotta façade from the Medical Arts Building that was demolished to make way for the new tower. The First National Center features three fountains — two inside the building and one outside — and a 60-foot glass winter garden in the lobby. The building's façade features a granite exterior.

The American flag hangs from the west side of Omaha's Woodmen of the World building, located at 1700 Farnam Street.

Among Woodmen's many programs benefiting the community is the Honor and Remembrance tribute, which pays respect to the heroes and victims of the September 11, 2001 terrorist attacks. As part of the program, Woodmen delegates have donated flagpoles and American flags to schools, fire departments, parks, and other public places. More than 2,400 Honor and Remembrance ceremonies have been held since the program began in 2002.

To mark the 5th anniversary of the attacks, Woodmen displayed two 50- by 100-foot U.S. flags on the tower of its 30-story building. Twin beams of light illuminated this scene in the Omaha skyline each evening during that remembrance week paying tribute to the victims at the World Trade Center.

Kutak, Rock and Campbell law firm acquired this classically styled building in 1977 for its offices. Located at 17th and Farnam streets, the New York architectural firm of McKim, Mead and White designed this structure in 1889 employing the Renaissance Revival style. At that time, its 10 stories qualified it as the tallest building in Omaha.

Built to resemble a Florentine palazzo, it has rusticated granite at the ground level exterior while the three lower floors are Massachusetts brownstone. The upper stories are hydraulic pressed brick.

Famous sculptor Louis Saint-Gaudens designed the large bronze eagle located on a pediment above the arched entrance.

Omaha National Bank purchased the building in 1909, and in 1920 an 11th story was added. Following World War II, an outer court was built to create additional offices over the second and third levels.

When Kutak, Rock and Campbell acquired the building, its interior was significantly redesigned while the exterior facade remained unchanged. It is listed on the National Register of Historic Places.

Few among today's Omaha citizens know that when the Blackstone Hotel was built, it was designed to be a family or residential hotel removed from the unending traffic of our central business district.

Located at 302 South 36th Street, Bankers Realty Investment Company built the Blackstone. F.W. Fitzpatrick served as its architect, and designed the structure in the Second Renaissance Revival style.

Charles Schimmel purchased the building in 1920 and converted the Blackstone into a regular hotel. It soon became known for its elegance and gained a reputation nationwide as the premier hotel between Chicago and San Francisco along the Lincoln Highway. Maintaining a fleet of Pierce-Arrow limousines for dignitaries arriving by train, the hotel became famous. A magnificent ballroom, rooftop gardens, and award-winning restaurants added to its prominence.

The hotel was renovated into offices in 1984 and renamed the Blackstone Center. In 2007, Peter Kiewit Sons', Inc., announced its purchase of the Blackstone, anticipating the company would use the entire building.

THE END OF AN OLD TRADITION, AND THE BEGINNING OF A NEW CHAPTER

Omaha's Rosenblatt Stadium hosted the famed College World Series beginning in 1950. The event moves to a new home, TD Ameritrade Park, in 2011.

A campaign by a dedicated group of Rosenblatt fans to save the stadium was long and fierce. They went to bat for Rosenblatt! Leading Omaha sculptor John E. Lajba created "The Road to Omaha" sculpture at the entrance to Rosenblatt Stadium, and it since has become a landmark for fans of the series. Lajba's sculpture will move to the new stadium once it opens.

OMAHA UNION STATION

Now known as the Durham Museum, the Art Deco building was originally named the Omaha Union Station. Peter Kiewit and Sons of Omaha built the station in 1931. Gilbert Stanley Underwood, a Los Angeles architect, designed this magnificent edifice. Its solid framework of structural steel on concrete pilings has endured to this day. The exterior cream-colored, glazed terra cotta tile continues to draw visitors' attention to its beauty.

The station closed in 1971 when Union Pacific ended its passenger service. The Union Pacific Corporation donated the building to the city of Omaha in 1973. Operating now as the Durham Museum, those who enter its doorway may once again be thrilled to view its main waiting room of light colored pine and oak wood trim along with black Belgian marble wainscoting. The terrazzo floor witnessed thousands of U.S. Military men and women who fought for our freedom during World War II and the Korean War. John E. Lajba's bronze sculptures recapture those moments before departure; Robert T. Reilly's dramatic script is retold through recordings telling the story of each statue. Children visiting from various schools are amazed at the Belgium blue marble colonnades flanking the 10 large stained plate glass windows. The 60-feet-tall ceiling supports six 2,000-pound crystal and bronze chandeliers.

A striking example of public architecture is seen in the Douglas County Courthouse at 17th and Farnam streets. Omaha architect John Latenser, Sr., designed the building and construction began in the spring of 1909. Considered to be one of Latenser's most significant buildings, the courthouse architectural style is French Renaissance Revival constructed on a steel frame. The walls were made of Bedford limestone on a granite base. A remarkable atrium ascends 110 feet and features a double skylight. The dome is enhanced with large mural panels conveying the artistic beauty of its rich interior. The terrazzo floors remain and most of the fine marble wainscoting on the walls and stairways are intact.

The courthouse was named in honor of Illinois Senator Stephen A. Douglas. In 1854, Omaha was in the geographic center of eight counties when Acting Governor Thomas B. Cuming issued a proclamation requiring election for members of the Territorial Legislature. Omaha was then chosen as the capital due to its central location. When Nebraska was admitted to the Union in 1867, the capital was moved to Lincoln.

This photo is of the third courthouse built in Omaha. The first dates back to the two-story structure in 1858. When the county outgrew the space, a second courthouse was built in 1885; it accommodated the county's needs for more than 25 years. Latenser was hired in 1908 to design a replacement for the second courthouse. His building opened in 1912. The courthouse earned listing on the National Register of Historic Places. The building continues to serve the community efficiently, with the Douglas County Civic Center added to the west side of the courthouse.

June 1912 saw the groundbreaking of this building, located at 20th and Douglas Streets, now known as the Omaha Scottish Rite Masonic Center. The Omaha Valley of Scottish Rite has been in the community since it was chartered in 1885.

The building was constructed from 1912 to 1914, with John Latenser, Sr., as its architect. Built in the Neoclassical Revival style, it features a Bedford limestone main exterior façade. Two majestic Ionic limestone columns that rise to the third floor draw attention to the north side of the building, formerly the front entrance to the Masonic Center.

The center has four floors and an attic; its interior features beautiful oak woodwork, marble, and terrazzo. It measures more than 47,000 square feet and is used for offices, a dining room, and a large ballroom. Additionally, the third floor has ceremonial rooms and an attractive 400-seat theater; the organ, installed in 1926, is among the largest in Omaha. A library and storage areas dominate the fourth level.

A "grand survivor" of another era, the Storz Mansion offers a unique view of an opulent time in Omaha's past. Built by Mr. and Mrs. Gottlieb Storz, brewing magnate and parents of Arthur C. Storz, the turn-of-the-century structure on Omaha's famed Gold Coast has been described by *American Preservation Magazine* Assistant Editor Janet Nyberg Paraschos a "one-of-a-kind Nebraska mansion."

Home to three generations of the Storz family, all the dignity, grandeur and elegance of the mansion still is alive, a rare tribute to the fine craftsmanship of those days of the early 20th century.

"From the stunning Tiffany-glassed dome skylight in the solarium, to the dazzling crystal chandeliers in the music room, to the beer and wine stube from the Trans-Mississippi Exposition of 1898 in the west courtyard, the Storz Mansion is an open door to another era in our history, a living tribute to the community and state."
– Arthur C. Storz, Jr.

Architects Fisher and Lawrie designed the mansion, which was built in 1905 at 3708 Farnam Street. This Jacobethan Revival style home is listed on the National Register of Historic Places and has been designated an Omaha Landmark.

Some years ago it appeared the mansion would be razed. A number of concerned citizens rallied around Art Storz, Jr., in his successful effort to save the home. Today it is still a family residence.

Architect John McDonald designed the Joslyn Castle in 1903. The castle's architecture is an impressive Scottish Baronial style. It is located in Omaha's Gold Coast Historic District at 3902 Davenport Street, and was added to the National Register of Historic Places in 1972. It received an Omaha landmark designation in 1979. Owned by the state of Nebraska, the castle is open to the public for tours at designated times and is available for special events. The Ramsey home in Dundee is also a John McDonald work.

Sioux Warrior by Matthew Placzek

The Joslyn Art Museum was a gift to the people of Omaha in 1931 from Sarah H. Joslyn as a memorial to her husband, George A. Joslyn. John and Alan McDonald designed the Art Moderne/Egyptian Revival building, with Georgia Pink marble on its exterior. The interior includes a handsome fountain court and numerous galleries designed with 38 types of marble obtained from quarries throughout the world.

The museum's Peter Kiewit Foundation Sculpture Garden, opened in the summer of 2009, features statues by local and national artists, in a setting enhanced with a reflecting pool and waterfall.

When Jonas L. Brandeis arrived in Omaha, he opened a store on South 13th Street. Its success motivated him to open another store at 16th and Douglas streets in 1888. That was a successful venture as well. By 1905, the J. L. Brandeis and Sons Company envisioned a larger, more permanent building. They selected John Latenser, Sr., to prepare the plans in the Second Renaissance Revival style for an eight-story structure at 16th and Douglas streets. It drew customers throughout the region to fulfill their desire to shop in a building that measured an entire block in length and a half-block in width.

Its steel frame was faced with Bedford limestone, brick, and terra cotta. The interior provided shoppers convenience, comfort, and unlimited options. Two more floors added in 1921 offered even more selections.

Its window displays were often works of art that passers-by could not resist, especially during the Christmas season. When they entered the first floor, people of all ages were in awe of the large fluted Corinthian columns that lent stability and trust to potential buyers.

A notable retail decline in downtown Omaha caused the store to close in 1980. A developer bought the property and converted the first two floors to commercial activity while the upper floors were renovated into office space. It also currently offers apartment space and condos. Despite the many changes over the years, the building's exterior continues to maintain its dominance in the downtown area.

Elmwood Tower was formerly known as the Masonic Manor. Located at 801 South 52nd Street in midtown Omaha, the 320-foot high-rise that stands 21 stories tall is the third tallest skyscraper in the city, behind only the First National Bank Tower and Woodmen Tower. This independent living facility features residential apartments for people age 50 and older.

One of Omaha's architectural classics was the Old City Hall, also known as the "Red Castle," located at 18th and Farnam streets in Omaha.

Omaha architect Charles F. Beindorf won an 1889 architectural competition, and shortly after the firm of John F. Coots, from Detroit, Michigan, began construction. The building, designed in Richardson Romanesque/Gothic Revival style, was completed in 1891.

The building's features included a raised basement and first floor built of granite and the use of red sandstone for floors two through five. Solid oak lined every interior wall. There were murals by artist Gustave Fuchs throughout the building. "Birdcage" elevators, added in 1916, brought visitors to the sixth floor of the building. Marble stairs from the main entrance led to the second-floor atrium court. An exterior clock tower almost 20 stories tall was added to the southwest corner of the building. A towering roof crowned the structure. Numerous gargoyles adorned the exterior, as well.

Mayor James C. Dahlman ordered the destruction of the top section of the tower in 1919. The building was renovated in 1950, which resulted in the loss of the original façade. By 1962, the Omaha Public Works director classified the building as dangerous. Consequently, in 1966 Mayor A. V. Sorensen sold it to Woodmen of the World. Demolition of the building took place later that year, along with the historic Bee Building to the east.

This photo is looking northeast. To the east of the city hall is the 19-story Woodmen of the World Building at 17th and Farnam streets. Across 17th Street to the east sits the impressive Omaha National Bank Building, which is now the Omaha Building due in large part to Kutak Rock law firm.

Ultimately, a new Woodmen of the World headquarters would rise 30 stories tall on the site. The Omaha National Bank moved into the Woodmen Tower along with other leading business and legal offices. WOW Radio and Television had offices on the first and second floors of the former Woodmen Building.

On May 25, 1965, Municipal Judge Paul J. Hickman administered the oath of office to Mayor A.V. Sorensen and seven members of the City Council: returning councilmen H. F. Jacobberger, Arthur D. Bradley, Jr., and Al Veys, and new representatives Robert G. Cunningham, Betty Abbott, Lynn R. Carey, and Sam Vacanti.

These pictures allow the viewer to appreciate Gustave Fuchs' wall murals used throughout the Old City Hall. Solid oak lined every interior wall along with complementary decorative lighting. Not seen are the "birdcage" elevators that brought visitors to the sixth floor of the building, as well as the marble stairs from the main entrance that led to the second floor atrium court.

Approximately 400 people, including local newspaper reporters and television crews, attended this historic event in the artistic Council chamber at the Old City Hall.

Photos: William W. Kratville

KIEL HOTEL

The Kiel Hotel in Council Bluffs, located at Fifth Avenue and South Main Street, attracted patrons and interest over the years. The Kiel Hotel reportedly opened in August 1877, when Council Bluffs native Henry Spetman joined Gottlieb Kiel and his stepson, Richard Hoist, in building and operating the hotel. It had been closed for a few years when the Boedicker family purchased it in 1922. Agnes McKay, a member of the family, managed the hotel until her death in 1980.

In 1982, Bob Edwards, president of Key Real Estate, bought the property and began renovation as part of the historic Haymarket area restoration. Twelve thousand square feet of office space were planned for the first two floors, with four apartments planned for the third level. The popular Duncan's Café, located in the building, remained after undergoing extensive remodeling. The café had been the hotel bar for many years.

A particular attraction on the first floor of the Kiel Building is the watercolor gallery featuring famous Council Bluffs landmark buildings and churches. The 12 framed pieces are the creative work of Hans Nielsen, Council Bluffs native and prominent artist.

The Greater Council Bluffs Board of Realtors recognized Bob and Norma Edwards for their restoration and preservation efforts. The Edwards had lived in a third-floor apartment when the work was completed in 1987. Both are now deceased.

Max Mohn, a German immigrant, arrived in Council Bluffs in 1869. He first worked as a shoemaker, and by 1879 he was listed in the city directory as the proprietor of the Creston House on South Main Street. That building is across the street from the current Council Bluffs City Hall site. In 1879, it was the location of the city's first Catholic Church.

The 1880-1881 Council Bluffs and Pottawattamie Directory described the building as a stone-fronted, three-story structure with 28 sleeping rooms. An 1884-1885 directory reported that the Creston House had completed a three-story, $15,000 addition that accommodated 47 more rooms. The building also had a dining room and offices and featured steam heat. In 1899, it claimed to be the only hotel among the dozen or more in the city that had fire escapes.

The last listing for the Creston House was in 1941, with E. E. Clark named as the proprietor. The following year, the Veterans of Foreign Wars was listed at 215 South Main Street. A supermarket operated at the location for about 25 years. The elegant old hotel looks like new in 2010, with its name and opening year emblazoned on its façade, reminding passersby of its original dignity.

A dedicated group of Council Bluffs citizens, the Historic Broadway Restoration Committee, is on its way to saving the city's earliest business district. The buildings on West Broadway stretch from First Street to Fourth Street. Richard "Dick" Miller exudes optimism for the future of the project.

Twenty-two business and service firms operate in the lineup of 1800 buildings. Having secured the district's support for historical designation from the city of Council Bluffs and the state of Iowa, the committee has succeeded in its initial efforts to revitalize and rehabilitate Historic Broadway, which reflects the rich heritage of the original business district of Kanesville/Council Bluffs. The photo, looking to the northeast on Broadway, features the area's new lighting, trees, decorative landscaping, and benches. Broadway United Methodist Church can be seen to the right.

Photos of the new Bayliss Park, dedicated in April 2007. Brower Hatcher, internationally recognized artist and sculptor, said, "As the heart of Council Bluffs, Bayliss Park is the perfect showcase for the revival and embodiment of this community's vitality."

The fountain stands as the centerpiece of the park's renovation and replaces the original one, installed in the 1880s. The performance pavilion provides an active amenity for the park that invites community performances, weddings, ceremonies and celebrations. To maintain continuity within the park, Brower included public seating in a quadrangle surrounding the fountain, applying the aesthetic of his sculpture to the chairs, tables, and benches.

Dolores D. Silkworth, landscape architect with RDG Planning & Design, brings a strong depth of experience, great enthusiasm, and energy to a project team. She is committed to improving the landscape environment both large and small. These characteristics are evident in the Bayliss Park project, on which the RDG design team worked collaboratively with the community to conduct public surveys to learn what citizens wanted in the park. Silkworth said that during the project's initial meetings, which included Ronald Hopp, former director of Council Bluffs Parks, Recreation and Public Property, and Council Bluffs Mayor Thomas P. Hanafan, they decided to conduct a master planning process. "Marty Shukert, a planner with RDG, and I arranged a series of meetings with our citizens and steering committees. RDG's collaborative team approach was very refreshing and absolutely appropriate."

St. John Church, on the campus of Creighton University, was designed by architect Patrick J. Creedon and built in the Gothic Revival style. With the cornerstone laid in 1887, the main part of the church was completed in 1888. However, it was not until 1922 that funding became available to hire architect Jacob Nachtigall to resume construction.

By 1927 the church, with the exception of the right tower, was complete. A large share of the donations came from the family of John A. Creighton, loyal and generous supporters throughout their lives and in their estates. The steeple was added in 1977 in keeping with the original design.

The thousands of students attending Creighton University over the decades have cherished this house of worship in their midst. Many graduates have returned to be married at St. John Church, a sacred edifice drawing many to prayers of gratitude and remembrance.

Morrison Stadium is a soccer-specific stadium located at Creighton University. It is named for the Rev. Michael G. Morrison, S.J., the beloved former president of Creighton University from 1981 to 2000. Earlier, Fr. Morrison had taught at Creighton Prep from 1967 to 1970, when at age 39 he became academic vice president at Creighton University. During his term, Fr. Morrison was often seen sitting on a bench interacting with university students who considered him a confidant and friend.

The stadium, designed by the architectural firm DLR Group, was opened in August 2003. It was called Creighton Soccer Field and became home to the Creighton Bluejays men's and women's soccer teams. In the fall of 2004, the facility was renamed Michael G. Morrison, S.J., Stadium. With a capacity of more than 6,000, the stadium also hosts non-soccer events such as concerts, the Omaha Symphony, and the opening ceremonies for Nebraska Special Olympics.

The stadium also hosted the state of Nebraska's first international friendly match on July 13, 2010. Women's national soccer teams of Sweden and the United States played to a 1-1 draw. The attendance was 6,493, which broke all previous records for a soccer match in Nebraska.

The Rev. Michael G. Morrison, S.J., president of Creighton University for 19 years, the longest term for a Creighton president, led the university during its most dramatic development and growth up to that time. Fr. Morrison saw thousands of young men and women from around the world secure a value-centered Jesuit education to help prepare them for careers and responsible citizenship.

Through a successful Creighton University 2000 capital campaign, Creighton continued to expand its potential for good and to capture high ranking as an institution of educational excellence.

Fr. Morrison has one characteristic that has set him apart from other Creighton leaders. He enjoys meeting Hilltop students in front of the Administration Building. He is pictured here with student Beth Conradson from Milwaukee, Wisconsin.

One of the city of Omaha's most beautiful churches and favorite marriage venues is Saint Margaret Mary at 61st and Dodge streets. The Ramseys have been parishioners since 1971.

The second pastor, the Rev. Joseph A. Suneg, an immigrant from Austria, designed many aspects of the church still admired today. In the late 1930s, he purchased 6.5 acres for the new church. At the time, church services were held in a building near 50th Street and Underwood Avenue in Dundee.

The new church was dedicated in 1941. Fr. Suneg worked closely on the plans and Leo A Daly architects designed the English Gothic style of architecture; it was constructed of Indiana limestone and oak.

Fr. Suneg created much of the artwork inside the church, including original carved statues. He also landscaped the grounds before the church was built, so that when the construction was completed the edifice would look as if it had been there for many years. When he died in May 1989, Monsignor Suneg left a legacy of beauty and dedication for the Archdiocese of Omaha in the building of St. Margaret Mary Church.

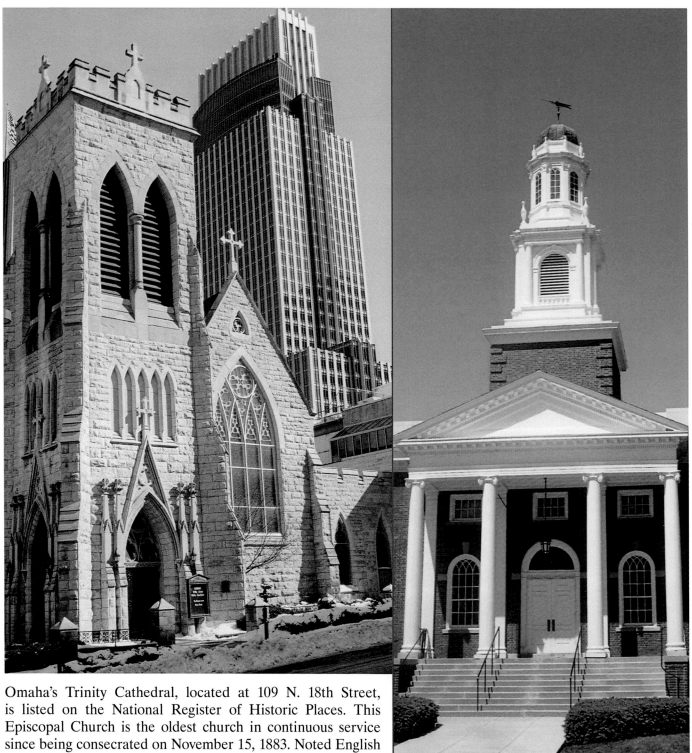

Omaha's Trinity Cathedral, located at 109 N. 18th Street, is listed on the National Register of Historic Places. This Episcopal Church is the oldest church in continuous service since being consecrated on November 15, 1883. Noted English architect, Henry G. Harrison, designed the church in the Late Gothic Revival in 1880 with rock-faced masonry walls and stone tracery over more than 43 stained glass lancet windows. The church was made with bluestone from Illinois; its design is cruciform with an entry tower extending outward. More than six stone crosses at various points of the roofline complement the exterior of the building.

The building in the background of the photograph is One First National Center, commonly known among Omahans as the First National Tower. This 45-story building, located at 16th and Dodge streets, is the city's tallest structure.

The First Unitarian Church of Omaha, located at 3114 Harney Street, earned National Register of Historic Places designation in 1980. Father and son partners, John and Alan McDonald, were the architects for this place of worship, dedicated in 1918. Former President William Howard Taft officiated at the laying of the cornerstone ceremony in 1917. The building is an outstanding example of Colonial Revival architecture featuring a welcoming double door entrance flanked by round arched windows.

More than 32 million people visit the Union Station in Washington, D.C., annually. It is the headquarters of Amtrak and is served by Amtrak, the MARC Train Service and Virginia Railway Express lines, commuter railroads, and the Washington Metro Transit system of buses and subway trains. Architect Daniel Burnham incorporated a number of different architectural styles into this structure. On October 27, 1908, the Union Station opened with the arrival of the Baltimore and Ohio passenger train from Pittsburgh. The terminal soon became the portal to the Capitol. During World War II, approximately 200,000 people passed through its doors in a single day.

Lincoln Monument, circa 1919. Located at Lafayette Avenue near Fairview Cemetery in Council Bluffs, this stately pylon was erected in 1911 and commemorates the place where Abraham Lincoln stood in 1859 to view and select the site for the eastern terminus of the nation's first transcontinental railroad.

Photo: Art Rogers Postcard Collection
Courtesy: R.H. Fanders

LEWIS & CLARK
MONUMENT
AND SCENIC OVERLOOK

This handsome structure honors the expedition of Lewis and Clark in 1804. Visitors may take North 8th Street in Council Bluffs to 19962 Monument Road to enjoy this historical site. It was part of the Lewis & Clark National Bicentennial Celebration in 2004. The city of Omaha is seen in the distance.

Enjoying Scenic Vistas

Some thoughts always find us young, and keep us so. Such a thought is the love of the universal and eternal beauty.

—Ralph Waldo Emerson

Seeing the Cliffs of Moher, Ireland's greatest tourist attraction, in 1988 proved to be an absolute delight. Located in Doolin in County Clare, West Ireland, this outstanding coastal feature ascends to more than 700 feet and extends south for close to five miles to Hag's Head. The vertical cliffs, with their steep drop into the choppy Atlantic Ocean, offer a haven for seabirds.

My first trip to Europe was in 1988, when Pat and I joined Bob and Jean Reilly on the Reilly-Flynn tour of London and Ireland. It was a marvelous journey where photo opportunities abounded. This picture is of O'Brien's Tower, County Clare, on the west coast of Ireland. The stone edifice is on a knoll that overlooks the famed Cliffs of Moher. Bob Reilly, an Irish expert of the first order, was walking down from the Lookout post. I had one exposure left in my camera and asked him to strike a dramatic pose. It turned out to be one of my best portraits. Jean Reilly liked it, too, and ordered prints for each family member. If you would like, I could take your photo in this same locale. Of course, you would have to pay my travel expenses!

O'Brien's Tower was built in 1835 by Cornelius O'Brien, a descendant of Brian Boru and the Kings of Thomand. It served as an observation point even then when hundreds of tourists visited the Cliffs.

Dingle Bay is located in County Kerry, western Ireland, along the Atlantic coast. On the north side of the bay is the colorful harbor town of Dingle where there are many opportunities for tourists to hear traditional Irish music, especially in the summer season. The town features a number of pubs along with restaurants and cafés. Many like to visit Dingle's aquarium and the art and craft shops. Tourism, fishing, and agriculture remain Dingle's principal industries.

Beginning in 1984, a bottlenose dolphin has made his presence known in the Dingle harbor area. Given the name *Fungi*, he has become a major attraction, showing up when tour boats carry enthusiastic passengers to meet him. Estimates of his age conclude he was born in the 1970s; the life span for his species is 25 years. The bottlenose dolphin standards conclude, he would now be considered as very old.

I could not resist taking this photo at the Columban Fathers weekend retreat at their mission headquarters in Bellevue, Nebraska, many years ago. Some of the men in attendance enjoyed walking throughout the grounds during our break periods. It provided an opportunity to reflect on the spiritual messages offered during the weekend.

A photographer friend who has improved several of my less-than-perfect photos presented me with this sweeping vista of our blossoming community. Terry Koopman, owner of Photographics, is nestled in his studio in the impressive Hot Shops Art Center at 1301 Nicholas Street. Koopman has made me look good many times over the years. Thanks, Terry, for this dramatic look at my second hometown.

TD Ameritrade Park under construction

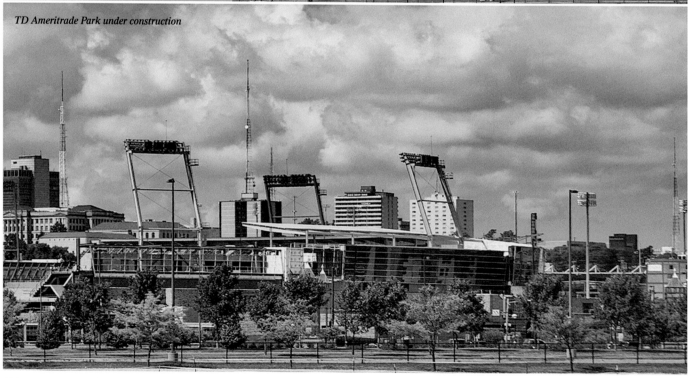

A racehorse named *Omaha* is revered in the annals of Aksarben history. Owned and trained by William Woodward, Sr., in 1935 *Omaha* became just the third Triple Crown Winner. As a 3-year-old, *Omaha* won the Belmont Stakes with prior wins in the Kentucky Derby and the Preakness. When he raced in England, *Omaha* won the Victor Wild Stakes and the Queen's Plate as a 4-year-old.

Omaha died in 1959 and was buried at the former Aksarben racetrack. This memorial was preserved and is displayed near the Aksarben Tower at Stinson Park with this inscription:

OMAHA
ONE OF THE IMMORTALS OF
THE AMERICAN TURF

Stinson Park at Aksarben Village in Omaha provides visitors with an amazing choice of venues. Located at 67th and Center streets, site of the former Aksarben racetrack, Aksarben Village is home to revitalized residential, retail, academic, business, and retail establishments.

One of the location's delightful attractions is the charming 4.5-acre Stinson Park, which provides open green spaces along with a performance stage. During the summer passersby can enjoy free entertainment options; everything from movies to live band performances. Attendees may pack a picnic supper, bring lawn chairs, and enjoy the evening's show.

The 100-foot-tall Aksarben Tower invites children to enjoy running through a play area at the base, which features water jets that are irresistible.

The official opening of the park was held in June 2009. Aksarben Future Trust board members were present; the site was named for the board's chairman Ken Stinson. They gathered around the new pillar, similar in design to the original Aksarben Tower. Jay Noddle, president of Noddle Companies, said that visitors really like this part of the city. "People are pleasantly surprised at how much is already here and how it's woven into the community," he said.

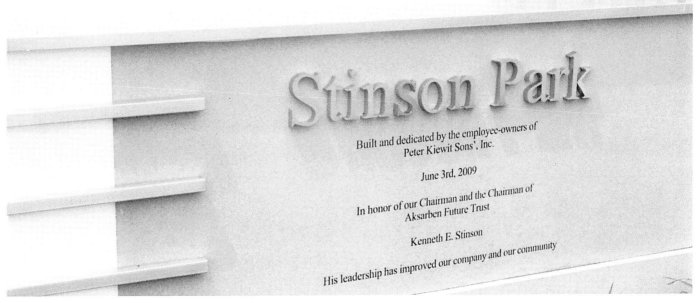

Bruce R. Lauritzen, chairman of First National Bank, said that Omaha's two sculpture parks — Pioneer Courage Park and Nebraska's Wilderness Park — were very special to him and his family.

I took these three photos at Pioneer Courage Park. Sculptors Blair Buswell of Highland, Utah, Ed Fraughton of South Jordan, Utah, and Kent Ullberg of Corpus Christi, Texas, created the statues of the four pioneer families heading westward from Omaha.

A creative team of artists and planners discovered a way to unite the two parks: Visitors at 14th Street and Capitol Avenue become part of the Pioneer Courage Park as the wagon train begins to leave Omaha. They see that the movement upsets a group of bison that starts stampeding down 15th Street and head for Dodge Street. Arriving at 16th and Dodge, the herd cause a flock of geese enjoying the pond at the Spirit of Nebraska's Wilderness Park to take flight after the cattle stampede into their territory. The majestic Canadian geese fly into and through the First National Tower Winter Garden Atrium.

Buswell has combined his love for art and sport in sculpting; since 1963, he has sculpted more than 60 busts of Pro Football Hall of Fame inductees. Fraughton is also an artist, sculptor and inventor, and his works relate to the history of the American West. Ullberg is a native of Sweden who now resides in Texas. This world-renowned artist created the American bison and the giant Canadian geese.

These sculptures and the area in which they reside represent one of the largest artistic installations of bronze and stainless steel in the world. Lauritzen has dedicated these two parks to the future generations of Omaha with the hope that they would enjoy them as much as he does.

Two scenic pictures taken near Jackson Hole, Wyoming, in the 1970s. The Grand Teton, its elevation of 13,775 feet making it the highest mountain in Wyoming's Grand Teton National Park, provides a breathtaking view for travelers. I took these photos while on a driving tour of the West with our children.

The Grand Canyon is one of the premier attractions in the world, counting more than 5 million visitors annually. Its overwhelming size and intricate, colorful landscape preserve significant geologic history; the rock layers serve as a record of the early geologic history of the North American continent. The canyon is 277 miles long, approximately 18 miles wide, and has a depth of more than one mile. Its south rim is 7,000 feet above sea level.

The Colorado River set its course 17 million years ago and continues to erode and form the canyon as it is seen today. The Grand Canyon National Park was established by an Act of Congress and signed into law by President Woodrow Wilson on February 26, 1919.

We decided to visit Winter Park, Colorado, during one of our family trips. We enjoyed the beauty of the mountains and experienced the highest incorporated town in the United States. Winter Park is a small town whose census figures in 2000 numbered the population at 662. That number changes significantly when seasonal work employees and tourists arrive.

Following a history of small settlements named Old Town and Hideaway Park, Winter Park was founded August 1, 1978.

In addition to skiing, visitors enjoy mountain biking in the Colorado Rockies, fishing, and hiking. Our family never ran out of options during our brief visit.

Respecting Historical Moments

There is no exercise better for the heart than reaching down and lifting people up.

—John Andrew Holmes

One of the most storied ventures of the Old West was the Pony Express Rider. Brenda J. Nilsen Daniher completed this magnificent sculpture in 2000. The piece is located at the park and rest stop at Julesburg, Colorado, just across the Nebraska border. It was dedicated May 25, 2002. The Pony Express Association and other benefactors sponsored the project.

This site became the home station for the Pony Express, which began at St. Joseph, Missouri, and Atchison, Kansas, ending in San Francisco. Its Nebraska station was near Fort Kearny. With all its romantic fame, the Pony Express lasted from April 3, 1860, to November 20, 1861 — just 19 months.

THE PONY EXPRESS TRAIL
1860 - 1861

OVERLAND CITY
(JULESBURG)

WALL OF REMEMBRANCE

Frances and Sam Fried at the Wall of Remembrance at Wyuka State Cemetery in Lincoln, Nebraska. The Heartland Holocaust Education Fund paid for this memorial wall; the images are from the Fried Family Private Collection. Sam Fried is a Holocaust survivor.

The Frieds are founders of the Heartland Holocaust Education Fund, a non-profit entity that partners with the Omaha Community Foundation and serves as a component of the Jewish Federation of Omaha Foundation. This program is perpetually funded for college-level Holocaust programs at universities and colleges. The founders and board members are dedicated to making an important difference to the lives of our future leaders as they gain greater understanding of the lingering and serious impact of the Holocaust.

The endowment has funded Holocaust education courses for students at the University of Nebraska-Omaha, the University of Nebraska-Lincoln, the University of Nebraska-Kearney, Creighton University, and Wayne State College.

The "Star of Remembrance" sculpture stands 16 feet tall and is comprised of two triangle frames that form a three dimensional star. Depicted are the three stages of the Nazi war against humanity: isolation, deportation, and extermination. The sculpture sits in the middle of an amphitheater setting along Wyuka Cemetery's Memorial Drive and tells you the story: Sixty years ago, 11 million innocent people were murdered during the Holocaust. Morton Katz of Toronto, Canada, is the memorial's artist and designer. He said, "It is my deepest hope that someday, when future generations come to visit this Memorial, genocide will truly be an aberration of the past." The Nebraska Holocaust Education Fund paid for the memorial.

Council Bluffs native John E. Lajba is a nationally recognized artist whose sculptures bring his subject's persona to life in the labor-intensive and time-consuming process resulting in masterful works of art in bronze.

Lajba's dedication to the Veterans Plaza Memorial at Bayliss Park in Council Bluffs is consistent with his determination to capture the intangible spirit of a person, a place, or an event. Names of Pottawattamie County veterans who served and died for their country in wars from the Civil War to today's conflicts are engraved on this memorial's granite walls.

This photo features the statues of a grandmother pointing to the name of her husband who died in World War I, with her grandson standing beside her. The expressions in the faces of the man and woman at the far end of the wall reveal their pride as well as their solemn sense of loss. The viewer is drawn to the universality of our humanity; we expect these bronze figures to speak. We draw closer to hear their words of wisdom acquired through long days and nights of waiting and hoping.

Many visitors to this monument have said, "The statue of this woman looks just like my grandmother!"

The Ruth Anne Dodge Memorial is located at Lafayette and North Second streets in Council Bluffs. The daughters of Ruth Anne Dodge commissioned noted sculptor Daniel Chester French, creator of the Lincoln Memorial statue in Washington, D.C., to create a statue depicting the angel described in their mother's account of her dreams shortly before her death. The magnificent statue was dedicated in a private ceremony in March 1920.

The bronze sculpture was commissioned in 1917 in memory of the wife of General Grenville Dodge. Located near Fairview Cemetery, the angel in the prow of a boat, holding a vessel from which water flows, is the interpretation of a dream described by Ruth Anne Dodge on the three nights preceding her death. The right hand of the angel extends in a beckoning gesture, urging her to drink from an overflowing urn. After three encounters, the daughter said their mother drank "…water which gave me immortality," and died within a few hours. The memorial is listed on the National Register of Historic Places.

Harold W. "Andy" Andersen, standing next to the plaque, is the retired publisher of the Omaha *World-Herald.* He had asked Bob Reilly and me to help publicize the placement of historic plaques marking the largest gathering of Indians in the country in late summer, 1851.

The historic site of the Horse Creek Treaty (formally the Fort Laramie Treaty) between the U.S. Government and Native Americans is near Morrill, Nebraska. It was a hot day, June 12, 1995, when Andersen; Chuck Trimble, president of the Nebraska State Historical Society and its first Native American president; Larry Sommers, director of the Nebraska State Historical Society; and I headed west for the event. Andersen was responsible for the fitting tribute of the plaques.

HORSE CREEK TREATY INTO FOCUS

JUNE 12. 1995, WAS A HISTORIC DAY IN NEBRASKA. IT MARKED THE UNVEILING OF A TRIO OF NEW NEBRASKA STATE HISTORICAL SOCIETY PLAQUES THAT COMMEMORATE THE OCCASION OF THE LARGEST ASSEMBLY OF AMERICAN INDIANS EVER GATHERED TO PARLEY WITH THE WHITE MAN. THANKS IN LARGE MEASURE TO FORMER OMAHA WORLD-HERALD PUBLISHER, HAROLD W. (ANDY) ANDERSEN, THE HISTORIC SITE HAS FINALLY BEEN RECOGNIZED.

THE SITE, NEAR MORRILL, NEBRASKA, WAS THE LOCATION FOR THE PARLEY AND SIGNING OF THE FORT LARAMIE TREATY, BETTER KNOWN AS THE "HORSE CREEK TREATY." IT IS ESTIMATED THAT 8,000 TO 12,000 INDIANS, REPRESENTING 10 TRIBES, GATHERED AT THE CONFLUENCE OF THE NORTH PLATTE AND HORSE CREEK IN THE LATE SUMMER OF 1851. THE MEETING WAS TO NEGOTIATE A PEACE TREATY WITH REPRESENTATIVES OF THE UNITED STATES GOVERNMENT.

THE COMMEMORATION PROJECT BEGAN SOME SIX YEARS AGO WHEN THE REV. JOHN J. KILLOREN, S.J., THEN COMPLETING A BIOGRAPHY OF THE MISSIONARY JESUIT, FATHER DE SMET, ASKED ANDERSEN TO HELP ARRANGE FOR PROPER IDENTIFICATION OF THIS HISTORIC SITE. ANDERSEN DID MUCH OF THE WORK TO BRING THE PROJECT TO FRUITION. HE THANKED COMMUNITY LEADERS IN MORRILL, STATE GOVERNMENT OFFICIALS, IN PARTICULAR, GOVERNOR BEN NELSON, OFFICIALS OF THE STATE HISTORICAL SOCIETY, THE DEPARTMENT OF ROADS AND THE STATE TOURISM DEPARTMENT FOR THEIR SUPPORT IN THE PROJECT.

A FOOTNOTE: IT IS A BEAUTIFUL AS WELL AS HISTORIC SITE. I RECOMMEND IT HIGHLY. IT IS JUST WEST OF MORRILL AND NOT FAR FROM THE WYOMING LINE. ALTHOUGH THE OFFICIAL NAME IS THE FORT LARAMIE TREATY, THE SITE WAS MOVED 34 MILES EAST INTO NEBRASKA. THE MOVE WAS NECESSITATED BECAUSE THERE WAS INSUFFICIENT GRASS FOR THE TRIBAL HORSES AROUND THE FORT. THANKS, ANDY, FOR GIVING THE EVENT ITS PROPER PLACE IN HISTORY SO THAT ALL CAN APPRECIATE WHAT HAPPENED AT HORSE CREEK 145 YEARS AGO.

BILL RAMSEY ASSOCIATES, INC.

This marker was once located on the grass near the Korean War-Vietnam War memorial at Omaha's Memorial Park. It now resides on a cement base along the drive directly in front of the memorial. It reads as follows:

MEMORIAL PARK
ESTABLISHED TO HONOR THOSE HEROIC
OMAHANS WHO GAVE THEIR LIVES IN THE
SERVICE OF THEIR COUNTRY

DEDICATED JUNE 5, 1948
BY PRESIDENT HARRY S. TRUMAN

Dr. Jonas Salk, pioneering U.S. physician and bacteriologist, received the Father Flanagan Award in 1977. His development of the Salk vaccine saved hundreds of thousands of children from the dreaded epidemic of poliomyelitis in the 1950s. We toured the Boys Town campus; this picture is at the burial site of Father Flanagan in the Dowd Chapel where the founder's portrait is on display.

The Franklin Delano Roosevelt Memorial in Washington, D.C., is not only a tribute to the 32nd president of the United States (1933-1945), but also serves as a stirring reminder of the era of the Depression, the New Deal, and World War II. Landscape architect Lawrence Halprin had fond memories of Roosevelt and rose to the demands of this impressive creation. Four outdoor rooms, each containing a waterfall, depict his terms of office through the sculptures and works by Leonard Baskin, Neil Estern, Robert Graham, Thomas Hardy, and George Segal. Inspiring quotations remind us of the words written and spoken by Roosevelt during those troubled times. Managed by the National Park Service, the memorial earned inclusion on The National Register of Historic Places on May 2, 1997.

Visitors can find the memorial located along the Cherry Tree Walk, near the National Mall on the Western edge of the Tidal Basin. I am seated on a stone bench with Jim Mortensen, my friend from the Korean War era.

Prospect Hill Cemetery, located at 3202 Parker Street, is Omaha's pioneer cemetery. Established in 1856, the gravesites now number more than 15,000 and include names of Omaha's military, civic, and religious leaders. Today our street signs and parks bear their names. Byron Reed, an early Omaha real estate broker, bought the land and Jesse Lowe, the first mayor of Omaha, designated 10 acres for burial purposes in 1858. Over the years, the cemetery would grow to 35 acres. It is now owned by Forest Lawn Memorial Park. Prospect Hill Cemetery is a designated Omaha Landmark.

The handsome statue of John T. Paulsen honors his memory. Born in Ockholm, Germany, on April 25, 1837, he eventually settled in Omaha and became a leading citizen and a member of the Nebraska State Senate in 1889.

This is a photograph of the first grave marker in Prospect Hill Cemetery, founded by Byron Reed in 1858. The cemetery is the final resting place for many prominent citizens of Omaha, as well as veterans from the War of 1812. Also interred were 100 Civil War soldiers, some of whom died on active duty or while serving at Omaha Barracks (Fort Omaha) during the late 1800s.

Veterans Plaza Memorial in Council Bluffs, Iowa, located at Bayliss Park, was dedicated July 4, 2003. Chuck Hagel, Vietnam veteran and former U.S. Senator from Nebraska, was the keynote speaker.

The idea for the Memorial was advanced by Bill Derby, Gale Foutch, and the late Howard L. Cross, Sr. Dolores D. Silkworth served as landscape architect for the project, and John E. Lajba was the sculptor.

The capital campaign was headed by Council Bluffs Mayor Thomas P. Hanafan, honorary chairman, Richard W. Peterson and Bill Ramsey, co-chairmen of the steering committee, and Dr. Dan Kinney, campaign chairman. John Batt, Norma Faris, Ross Grego, Bob Hill, Ronald Hopp, Jon Leu, and Laural Ronk joined the aforementioned individuals on the project's steering committee.

Darlene McMartin, director of Veterans Affairs, Pottawattamie County, also served on the committee. Her staff researched names of those from the county who gave their lives for their country. Beginning with the Civil War and extending to the present day, the service men and women's names are inscribed on the granite wall.

The bronze statue of this mournful couple portrayed their grief at the burial of their child. They were part of a group of Mormons making their exodus from Nauvoo, Illinois, through Council Bluffs, and Omaha to reach the valley of the Great Salt Lake in Utah. Under the leadership of Brigham Young in 1847, the majority of Mormons arrived at their destination and settled there. Along the way, many died of exposure to the elements and lack of proper nourishment for themselves and their animals. Sculptor Avard Tennyson Fairbanks captured the sadness parents felt in the loss of a child. The statue resides at Omaha's "Winter Headquarters" Mormon Cemetery, Northridge Drive and State Street, where it was installed in 1951.

The Omaha Police Department has served our community since 1887. The OPD continues its mission of dedicated protection as it responds dutifully on the front lines every day, even as officers risk their lives to assure our safety. Names and dates of police officers killed in the line of duty are inscribed on the base of the memorial. Sculptor John E. Lajba reflects that heroism in the bronze statues he created and installed in 1994.

The citizens of Omaha honor these brave men and women and their families for their sacrifices that assure our safety and protection every hour of the day.

For more than a century, the Omaha Fire Department has honored those who have died in the line of duty. The first to be listed were four firefighters: John Lee, William McNamara, Alonzo Randall, and Lewis Wilson. They died on September 4, 1878, when the floor on which they stood collapsed in a building at 14th and Farnam streets.

The Omaha Firefighters Memorial at the Lewis and Clark Riverfront honors these men and all those brave men and women and their families for their service to our community. The four photographs of the memorial illustrate the beautifully landscaped site with its focus on "The Protector" by Matthew Placzek, local artist and sculptor. The bronze statue is appropriately named and reminds viewers of the heroism required of each firefighter who sets aside personal safety to rescue those in peril. The memorial was appropriately dedicated on September 11, 2009.

The surrounding pedestals hold bronze plaques listing the names of the fallen; a brick walkway carries the names of active and retired firefighters. Many dedicated hours from the citizens of Omaha and surrounding communities resulted in this inspiring and fitting tribute to our firefighters. Their contributions of personal time and monetary support transformed this space into a fitting place for remembrance and reflection.

U.S. Senator Ben Nelson and Capt. Darren Garrean of the Omaha Fire Department were among those attending the 9/11 observance ceremony in 2010 at the Omaha Firefighters Memorial. Fifty-five Omaha firefighters who had died in the line of duty were honored as their names were read aloud.

PROTECTOR
BY
MATTHEW PLACZEK
2009

The South Omaha Main Street Historic District is a work of art in progress. One of the most recent additions is appropriately named "Tree of Life," by public artist/sculptor David Dahlquist of RDG Planning & Design, Des Moines, Iowa.

Dahlquist said this piece of art celebrates the area's past and present, with its residents' historic past rooted in Croatia, Czechoslovakia, and Poland along with today's large Latino American community.

The metal sculpture pays homage to all these cultures.

Working with regional, community and notable city planners/designers such as Marty Shukert, Pat Dunn, Dolores Silkworth and others, Dahlquist and the South Omaha Business Association said they were interested in improving the infrastructure of South Omaha in a way that was directly related to this vibrant community. Former Omaha city planner, Robert "Bob" Peters, was also affiliated with the group.

Dedicated on April 29, 2010, the 37-feet-tall "Tree of Life," pedestaled on a large footing of concrete, has become the entrance to the historic district located at the southeast corner of 24th and L streets. Carol Bicak, *World-Herald* staff writer, wrote about this area that is on the National Register of Historic Places, "There is a profusion of impressive murals painted on walls in the area, even in alleyways. Sculptures and pottery sold in some of the shops make their way to the sidewalks to add color and interest to the business district."

The South Omaha Branch of the U. S. Postal Service is located at 24th and M streets. It was built around 1898 in a Classical Revival style with John Latenser as its architect. This attractive structure is one of the oldest post office buildings continuing to be used as a postal station. Early in its history, the building housed federal offices for agencies of the Agricultural Department and Department of Animal Husbandry.

The buff brick structure, trimmed with terra cotta, features giant columns supporting a projecting entablature and also has an arched entrance portal and pedimented window heads.

In May 1926, Peter Kiewit and Sons built the Livestock Exchange Building, the largest and most visually prominent structure in South Omaha. Architect George Prinz designed the centerpiece of the area in the Romanesque and Northern Italian Renaissance Revival styles. It was added to the National Register of Historic Places in 1999. The red brick building stood as the center of the thriving livestock industry in Omaha. The stockyards and meatpacking industry employed half of Omaha's workforce in 1957.

Originally, the building at 2900 O Plaza operated as a business and trading center. Surrounded with 260 acres of livestock pens, the Livestock Exchange Building rented space for offices, a bakery, and cafeteria as well as a telegraph center, apartments, and a convention hall.

The livestock industry saw major components of its business close, creating vacancies in this building for a number of years. When the building was converted to mixed use in 2005, it offered 100 apartments along with community and commercial space. The surrounding area is once again active with commercial, medical, and light industrial uses.

The Packers National Bank building has been located at 4939 South 24th Street since 1907. Originally established in 1891, the bank was closely affiliated to the Omaha Stockyards. Its early officers were executives in the meat packing industry.

Thomas Rogers Kimball designed this building in the Second Renaissance Revival style. The building was vacated in 1979 and eventually was converted into office and residential space. The structure remains in excellent condition with its unaltered façade of brick and decorative limestone trim. It is listed on the National Register of Historic Places and is part of the South Omaha Main Street Historic District on South 24th Street.

Main entrance to Wyuka Cemetery, a "Place of Rest," along with a funeral home and park. It is located at 3600 O Street in Lincoln.

This marker in Section 4 of Wyuka Cemetery recalls the talented singer and actor, Gordon MacRae. Many still enjoy watching reruns of the landmark musical movie, "Oklahoma;" several measures of that opening song, "Oh What a Beautiful Mornin'," are inscribed across the top of the polished black granite monument honoring his memory.

He was born in East Orange, New Jersey, and graduated from Deerfield Academy in 1940. During World War II, MacRae served as a navigator in the United States Army Air Force. By the mid-1940s, he was making recordings with Jo Stafford. After his first film in 1948, he and Doris Day appeared in several movies. His successful appearances in "Oklahoma" in 1955, and "Carousel," in 1956, placed him in the annals of movie history.

The quotation at the bottom of MacRae's cemetery marker is from President Ronald Reagan: "Gordon will always be remembered wherever beautiful music is heard."

Directly across the road from the Firefighters Memorial, at the north end of Section 3A, is a striking memorial with two red-painted symbolic steel I-beams signifying the World Trade Towers in New York City, destroyed by terrorists attacks on September 11, 2001.

IN MEMORY OF
THE MANY HEROES WHOSE LIVES WERE LOST
AND THE LOVED ONES THEY LEFT BEHIND
SEPTEMBER 11, 2001

God Bless America

TERRORIST ATTACKS CAN SHAKE THE
FOUNDATIONS OF OUR BIGGEST BUILDINGS,
BUT THEY CANNOT TOUCH
THE FOUNDATION OF AMERICA.
        -PRESIDENT GEORGE W. BUSH

NEBRASKA FIREFIGHTERS MEMORIAL

PROTECTORS OF LIFE
TEMPERED BY FIRE
REMEMBERED FOREVER

IN HONOR OF NEBRASKA'S FIREFIGHTERS AND THEIR FAMILIES

PAUSE HERE IN SILENCE
FOR THOSE WHO ANSWERED THE SIREN'S CALL

DEDICATED MAY 25, 2003

Memorial plaque for the World Trade Towers in Wyuka Cemetery.

One of the most prominent sculptures located in the eastern edge of Wyuka Cemetery is the Nebraska Firefighters Memorial, which is located at the south end of Section 41. The large bronze figure of a kneeling firefighter was sculpted by S. Mariami in 2001 and dedicated in honor of Nebraska's firefighters and their families on May 25, 2003.

Our back cover "umbrella couple" is actually Jim and JoAnn Mortensen, close friends of the Ramseys. They are from Vacaville, California, and frequently vacation with us. Here they are at the Korean War Memorial in Washington, D.C.

WASHINGTON MONUMENT

This monument, made of marble, granite and sandstone, is the world's tallest stone structure. Located in Washington, D.C., this obelisk stands 555 feet, 5 1/8 inches tall. Architect Robert Mills designed the monument; construction began in 1848. Political and monetary setbacks delayed the completed monument's dedication until 1885. Its official opening occurred on October 9, 1888.

Many visitors are unaware that two words are inscribed on the aluminum cap atop the Washington Monument: "Laus Deo," translated: "Praise be to God." The capstone was set on December 6, 1884. From that high point, one can readily see that the designer of the District of Columbia, Pierre Charles L'Enfant, planned a perfect cross on the landscape with the White House (north), the Jefferson Memorial (south), the U.S. Capitol (east), and the Lincoln Memorial (west).

Operation Detachment (February 1945) was a battle in which the United States fought for and captured Iwo Jima from the Imperial forces of Japan. The epic battle produced some of the fiercest fighting in the Pacific Campaign of World War II.

This photograph has a special meaning for me since it was a gift from George Paulson, a Marine survivor of that battle. Paulson is a fellow Council Bluffsian and a friend. He lost a leg to Japanese machine gun fire but went on to own a construction company in his hometown.

In 1976, Paulson was a national president of the Fifth Marine Corps Association whose national reunion was held in Omaha. The division was one of several Marine units that won that pivotal battle.

I was the public relations and development director at Boys Town at that time. Paulson called me and asked if officers from the division association might visit Boys Town and make a presentation to our director, Rev. Robert Hupp. Fr. Hupp was a naval chaplain on an aircraft carrier in World War II. With a resounding "Yes!" and "Semper Fi," Paulson and his fellow Marines were at our doorstep. They presented Fr. Hupp and me with a classic framed photograph of the war.

It had the division's autograph to make it even more special. Three of the six flag raisers were later killed on Iwo Jima: Harlon Block, Texas; Franklin Sousley, Kentucky; and Mike Strank, Pennsylvania. Survivors went home to lead a War Bond Drive, the most successful of World War II. They were: Ira Hayes, Arizona; Rene Gagnon, New Hampshire; and John Bradley, Wisconsin, a Navy Corpsman.

Marines on Mt. Suribachi, Iwo Jima, Feb. 23, 1945

ASSOCIATED PRESS NEWSPHOTO

BY JOE ROSENTHAL

Applauding Patriotism and the Military

Uncommon valor was a common virtue.

— Admiral Chester Nimitz, U.S. Navy

My favorite patriotic photo: "For God and Country." Mother Bernice Spores was a super patriot and a member of the Religious of the Sacred Heart Community at Duchesne when this picture was taken in the early 1960s. Mother Spores, in her 70s, had a daily routine in which she carried the American flag out of a three-story window along with a stepladder. She proceeded to climb the ladder and lean over the parapet to raise the colors. She returned at nightfall to take the colors down. This was a labor of love and went on for years. As the public relations director at Duchesne, I tracked down the story. It appeared on the front page of the Omaha *World-Herald*, whose photographer, Pat Hall, was my grade school and high school classmate. My photo was sent to the Freedoms Foundation at Valley Forge, where it received an award for patriotism.

Artist Stephen C. Roberts, born in Omaha, created this life-size mural, "Nebraska American Heroes," for the Norfolk Veterans Home, where it was installed in 2001. The painting features current or past veterans of various wars. As a Korean War Marine veteran, I am included in the mural (sans uniform) holding a treasured "box from home." U.S. Senators Ben Nelson and Chuck Hagel were special guests.

Roberts won a competition sponsored by the Nebraska Capitol Murals Commission. He painted the eight large murals in his art studio from 1992 to 1996. These were installed in the Memorial Chamber located on the 14th floor of the Nebraska State Capitol in Lincoln.

An interesting pair of photos that span more than 50 years. In May 2001, I traveled to the Republic of Korea for a third time resulting in this photo at the Demilitarized Zone at Panmunjom. The first was at the government's expense in 1951; the second time, at my own expense in 1978 following a Rotary International convention in Tokyo. This is the most heavily fortified frontier in the world. In the 1950s, the U.S. and United Nations forces crossed this divide between North and South Korea on many occasions as the war raged on for three years before an armistice was signed on July 27, 1953.

At the front in June 1951, during the Korean War with Able Company, First Battalion, Fifth Regiment, First Marine Division Reinforced. It was one of the rare quiet times in the combat zone. We were preparing to go on patrol. My equipment consisted of a cartridge belt, bayonet, canteen, M-1 rifle, and first-aid pouch. At my left foot was a case of hand grenades; the C-7 carton held our C-rations. A mountain looms in the background — in all backgrounds in Korea!

I left Korea November 17, 1951, wounded on patrol in North Korea. I was taken to a MASH unit, then to Japan, and finally to Oak Knoll Naval Hospital in Oakland, California, for 7 months. I recovered in late spring and was homebound on a Greyhound bus June 2, 1952.

Memorial Park, located at 6005 Underwood Avenue in Omaha, was created as a memorial tribute for all the men and women from Douglas County that have served in the armed forces. A local citizen proposed the idea and a group of community leaders and businessmen — Robert H. Storz, owner of Storz Brewery, and Henry Doorly of the Omaha *World-Herald*, the Omaha zoo namesake, among them — created the Memorial Park Association. This group raised the funds to erect a monument at a location near Omaha University.

President Harry S. Truman dedicated the site on June 5, 1948. Other groups sponsored enhancements to Memorial Park over the years: Omaha Rose Society added a rose garden in 1959; Woodmen of the World erected flagpoles and flags on the driveway at the park's entrance in 1990, as part of its centennial observance; and a pedestrian bridge over Dodge Street was completed in 1968. It is called Memorial Park Pedestrian Bridge.

Members of the U.S. Military are present for the tributes to veterans held throughout the year at Memorial Park in Omaha. A drummer in colonial costume appears at the top of the stairway

The Korea-Vietnam Peace Memorial was dedicated in 1976 at Memorial Park in Omaha. The monument honors the veterans of the two wars and is located in front of the World War II Memorial. Private funds were raised to create this tribute to the men and women who served in those wars. Names of those who died in the line of duty and those missing in action are engraved on bronze plaques.

I was among a group of citizens that began raising funds in 1970 to honor these veterans.

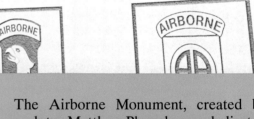

The dedication ceremony of the Airborne Monument in Heartland of America Park in downtown Omaha marks a proud moment for our community and its veterans.

For more than 7 years, the Heartland Airborne Memorial Association toiled to create a fitting tribute to the nation's fighting forces and veterans that would enhance Omaha as a premier meeting place for military veterans' conventions and reunions.

A lone paratrooper glides to the site of the ceremony. This dramatic jump, preceding the dedication ceremony, honored the living and deceased members of our nation's valiant warriors.

Internationally acclaimed Omaha artist Matthew Placzek created the inspiring bronze sculptor that features an airborne trooper preparing to jump from an aircraft. The monument also memorializes the members of our Armed Forces who have fallen in the line of duty in the War on Terrorism in Iraq and Afghanistan.

Many individuals and corporations gave generously of their time, talent, and treasure to honor the men and women of our Armed Forces. All were pleased that the famed 101st "Screaming Eagles" Airborne Division held its national reunion in Omaha at this historic time. I was proud to have served as a campaign coordinator for this worthy cause.

The Airborne Monument, created by sculptor Matthew Placzek, was dedicated at Heartland of America Park in Omaha on August 11, 2007. The dramatic memorial features an airborne trooper preparing to jump from an aircraft. The Airborne Monument serves as a testimonial to the persistence, patience, tireless work, and vision of Airborne veterans in our community and region who stayed the course and completed their mission. The Heartland Airborne Memorial Association sponsored this tribute. Many benefactors joined in the effort that resulted in a magnificent patriotic display for all to honor and enjoy.

Omaha hosted three legendry World War II airplanes in the summer of 2010: the B-17 Flying Fortress Heavy Bomber and the B-24 Liberator "Witchcraft," both famed bombers, and the P-51 Mustang "Betty Jane," a fighter plane from both World War II and the Korean War.

This event, held at TAC Air at Omaha's Eppley Airfield, was part of the Collings Foundation's "Wings of Freedom" tour, now in its 21st year. The tour's goal is to visit more than 100 cities annually.

This "Witchcraft" is the only flying B-24 left in the world. The names of hundreds of World War II Army Air Forces veterans are scrawled on the plane. Many people took advantage of the opportunity to sit where the gunners did, and some paid for a half-hour ride in the bombers.

Ironically, two heroic pilots who flew these classic aircraft in World War II were old friends. John Rickerson was a prominent Omaha attorney and major benefactor of the Omaha Home for Boys, where he and his two brothers were residents at one time. His B-17 was hit during a raid over Germany and crash-landed in France. The crew survived. I wrote a booklet on his life, "On a Wing and a Prayer — A Profile of John A. Rickerson," and every boy at the home was given a copy of this story.

Lloyd Kilmer, longtime Douglas County Clerk and Republican leader, was a pilot on a B-24 Liberator. His plane was shot down, and Kilmer was taken prisoner by German troops. NBC Nightly News anchor Tom Brokaw's classic book, "The Greatest Generation," featured Kilmer's experience.

B-17

P-51 MUSTANG

B-24

One of our area's most honored historic military bases is old Fort Crook, Offutt Air Force Base. This base was home to the Cold War nerve center, the Strategic Air Command, and today the U.S. Strategic Command.

In 1890, the War Department commissioned Fort Crook to serve as a U.S. Army Depot; it was located south of Bellevue, Nebraska, along the Missouri River, and was named for Major General George Crook, a Civil War veteran and Indian fighter.

By 1921, Fort Crook saw a new airfield take shape that would serve as a refueling stop for transcontinental flights. It became "Offutt Field," honoring Omaha native and World War I air ace 1st Lt. Jarvis Offutt, killed in 1918 while flying with the Royal Air Force.

Later, the Army Air Corps selected the Glenn L. Martin Company to use Offutt Field as the site of a new bomber plant in 1940. The Martin bomber plant churned out hundreds of B-29 Superfortresses and B-26 Marauders before World War II ended. The "Enola Gay" and "Bockscar" were built and modified here. They would drop the first atomic weapons in the cities of Hiroshima and Nagasaki, Japan in August 1945, which sealed the Allies' victory in World War II. Paul Tibbets personally chose the "Enola Gay" from the vast assembly line.

Nebraska Governor Dwight Griswold and Glen L. Martin escorted President Franklin D. Roosevelt on a tour of the plant on April 26, 1943. By 1948, Offutt Field, under the new Department of the Air Force, was named Offutt Air Force Base. Its facilities expanded dramatically as it became headquarters of the Strategic Air Command (SAC).

The government deactivated SAC during a reorganization of its military unit structure in 1992. What followed was the U.S. Strategic Command (USSTRATCOM), the Department of Defense Unified Combatant Command.

I took these photos at the north main gate, or Kinney Gate, at U.S. Strategic Command Headquarters. Rows of international flags fly along the boulevard to the gate. Standing as a symbol of America' superior air power is the legendary B-29 workhorse of the U.S. Air Force for so many years.

After 50 years of existence and following a successful $33 million capital campaign, the Strategic Air Command (SAC) held the groundbreaking ceremony for a new facility near Ashland, Nebraska, on March 22, 1996.

It was an exciting day in June 1997 when the SR-71 airplane was the first aircraft to leave the facility in Bellevue and travel 36 miles to its new home in Ashland. The SAC Memorial Society dedicated the new facility on Armed Forces Day, May 16, 1998, the 39th anniversary of the SAC Museum. In 2001, the society changed the name of the building to the Strategic Air and Space Museum.

Events at the Strategic Air and Space Museum have honored many veterans of various wars for their service to our country. These well-attended events provide opportunities for visitors to personally thank the heroic men and women who risked their lives to assure that the United States of America would remain the Land of the Free. Interim Director Evonne Williams, along with her husband, Bill Williams, organized the "Freedom Flights" for veterans to visit the World War II Memorial in Washington, D.C.

John Wayne, the "Duke," said he was honored to meet Marines preparing for the Korean War. In December 1950, I had arrived at Camp Pendleton, Oceanside, California, to begin advanced infantry training. I had been recalled for deployment with thousands of other GIs around the country. On a free Sunday afternoon, we visited the film set for "Flying Leathernecks," which was filmed at the base. Wayne and Robert Ryan were the stars. After shooting several scenes, they took a break and visited with us. They wished us well and thanked us for serving in this war. Another Marine took this photo.

From the left: Subby Zito, Omaha; Bill Ramsey, Council Bluffs; "The Duke," John Wayne; Keith Zimmer, Lexington, Nebraska; and Jerry McAtee of Davenport, Iowa

Ernie Pyle standing at the fountain in Bayliss Park in 1941. He was awarded a Pulitzer Prize in reporting in 1944 for his writing from the European battlefront during World War II. Pyle was killed in the Battle of Okinawa in the spring of 1945.

Photo: Council Bluffs Daily Nonpareil

This photo, taken at Camp Pendleton in Oceanside, California, in the 1970s, finds a Marine Corps Drill Instructor bellowing, "Listen up, you people!" The new recruits' ears were on high alert as the Drill Instructor directed them in demanding military terms. Compromise was not an option.

I took this photo as my son, Jim Ramsey, graduated at the Marine Corps Recruit Depot in San Diego, California, in the 1980s. Jim is in the middle of the first row. Pat and I, along with our daughter, Peggy, cheered loudly. I went through the same ceremony in March 1949.

Navy Commander Lloyd M. "Pete" Bucher, an alumnus of Boys Town, lived through a harrowing and historic experience when his ship, the USS *Pueblo* (AGER-2), was captured by North Korean ships in 1967. One sailor was killed; Bucher and his crew of 82 were taken prisoner. The incident resulted in almost daily news coverage during the tense negotiations to free the crew. They were held from 1967 to 1969. Bucher helped his crew survive captivity in North Korea. He died in 2004 at age 76 and is buried at Fort Rosecrans National Cemetery in San Diego, California.

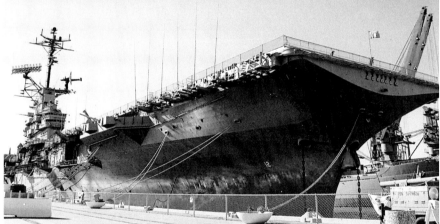

During World War II, the USS *Hazard* (AM-249) was an Admirable-class minesweeper serving in the United States Navy. It was fitted for wire and acoustic sweeping and could double as an anti-submarine warfare platform. This Admirable class of minesweepers was used for patrol and escort duties, which the USS *Hazard* completed when she escorted a convoy from San Francisco to Pearl Harbor. When the war ended, she cleared the seas off Korea and Japan for the occupation forces.

The USS *Hornet*, an Essex-class aircraft carrier, became the eighth ship to bear that name upon commission in November 1943 when the vessel joined the U.S. forces in the Pacific War.

She engaged in a number of battles during the conflict, and following the war returned troops back to the United States during an effort called Operation Magic Carpet. She also served in the Korean and Vietnam wars and helped recover astronauts as they returned from the Moon.

In 1970, the *Hornet* was decommissioned and later designated a National Historic Landmark. My wife and I made a stop to tour the USS *Hornet* Museum in Alameda, California; in 1998 the aircraft was opened to the public.

In 1946, the USS *Hazard* returned to the United States where she was decommissioned and joined the reserve fleet. A group of Omaha businessmen purchased the USS *Hazard* when she was stricken from the Navy Register in 1971. The USS *Hazard* is now on public display at Freedom Park near the waterfront in East Omaha.

On January 14, 1986, the USS *Hazard* was designated a National Historic Landmark. It is one of the best-preserved World War II warships in the United States.

Photo: Omaha World-Herald

I took this picture of Lieutenant John J. "Johnny" Parle's tombstone on the west side of the cemetery. The plaque pays tribute to his heroic act of courage.

One of the most unusual and dramatic acts of courage in World War II occurred at the hands of John J. "Johnny" Parle from Omaha, on July 10, 1943, as U.S. forces prepared to invade Sicily off the coast of Italy.

Ensign Parle, 23, was aboard LST 365, which would launch smaller boats for the invasion. They began swinging landing boats out, ready for lowering boat #5, loaded with explosives. A smoke pot in the boat became ignited accidentally. Nobody was in the boat. There was danger that the explosives could be ignited and many shipmates and troops would be killed or wounded and the mission could have been a disaster.

Parle leaped into boat #5, put out the fuse, grabbed the flaming smoke pot, and hurled it into the sea. His personal sacrifice probably saved the ship, the men, and the invasion. Parle died at a field hospital days later from the poisonous fumes he had inhaled. His body remained on foreign soil until May 1944. His casket was escorted by Navy Lt. Donald Ross for his wake and burial in Omaha at Holy Sepulchre Cemetery. This picture is of Parle's parents kneeling in prayer beside his casket and Navy Lt. Ross with a black armband standing at attention. Lt. Ross also received a Medal of Honor for his actions at Pearl Harbor December 7, 1941.

FLAG RAISING IWO JIMA

An amazing thing happened in the spring of 2008 when Bill and Evonne Williams undertook an impossible project — to transport World War II veterans to the nation's capital to view the recently installed World War II monument, the last major tribute on the Mall following the Vietnam and Korean War memorials.

With an overwhelming response from generous benefactors, funds were raised to begin the "Honor Flights" for the warriors who helped save the world from the Axis Powers. In all, four flights took more than 1,500 veterans to Washington, D.C. The Williamses supervised each flight and staffed every flight with volunteers who tended to the needs of the aging veterans, many with crutches and in wheel chairs. It was a small miracle!

Today Evonne Williams is interim director of the Strategic Air and Space Museum in Ashland, Nebraska. She is assisted by her husband, a dedicated staff, and an army of volunteers and generous benefactors.

The photo was taken on their first "Honor Flight," May 21, 2008. The Williamses are with World War II Marine veteran, Rich Lang, who was wounded on Guam. They are in front of the world's largest bronze memorial, the "Flag Raising at Iwo Jima" in February 1945. It was modeled after a photo taken by Associated Press photographer Joe Rosenthal. It is probably the most widely published icon representing the Allies' victory in World War II. Bill and Evonne, who have a "military family" of their own consisting of two Soldiers and two Marines, received the "Service Above Self" award from the Rotary Club of Omaha in 2009.

Three World War II Veterans relax in front of the Veterans Plaza Memorial. These members of the steering committee are (from left) Gale Foutch, Billy Derby, and Howard Cross. They asked me to join them in 2001 when they were attempting to raise funds to honor our veterans with a statue.

Gale Foutch

Billy Derby

Howard Cross

Richard W. "Dick" Peterson spoke at the annual July 4th ceremonies honoring all veterans at the Veterans Plaza Memorial in 2009. He is a World War II veteran and retired attorney living in Council Bluffs. Dick and I served as co-chairmen of the Veterans Plaza Memorial Steering Committee; Dr. Dan Kinney was campaign chairman, while Council Bluffs Mayor Tom Hanafan was our honorary chairman and assisted us in raising the necessary funds for this tribute to the men and women in the armed forces. The memorial plaza was dedicated in 2003.

Left: Mick Guttau, speaker, was a Cobra Helicopter aircraft commander in Vietnam

★★★★
The Glory of Their Spirit

When destiny demanded and country called,
they in answer left our rolling hills
and great river valley, and learned the arts of war.
Then, on and beneath restless waves of the deep,
in endless skies and across vast oceans to island shores,
on broad plains and barren hillsides, in dark forests,
on snow-covered mountains and in the rubble of smashed villages
and cities they faced and fought, with valor and dedication,
those who challenged our ideals and freedom and,
in the very vortex of combat, were then greeted and embraced by Death.

The soldiers, sailors, marines and airmen were not born
to die in the youth of their lives–yet they did.
They were not born to die death of violence–yet they did.
By cruel and brutal circumstances of war, they gave their lives
that we might live our lives and years in liberty and peace.

Never should we forget their ultimate sacrifice.

We now in their memory carve their names in stone,
and enshrine them in our hearts;
we now cast in eternal bronze, figures who in sorrow and
in the long, long thoughts of youth
reflect on the last measure of devotion given by those we now honor,
and we join their mute and motionless yet eloquent presence
in their silent meditation,

Thinking not only of the passing of the departed patriots,
But remembering the glory of their spirit.

– Richard W. Peterson

Two patriots and military veterans made presentations on Flag Day, June 15, 2010, at the Omaha-Douglas Civic Center Plaza. Brigadier General Jim Murphy, Nebraska Army National Guard, (Ret.), is at the microphone. Glenn Freeman, U.S. Air Force Chief Master Sergeant (Ret.), welcomed the audience as president of the Omaha Chapter of the Freedoms Foundation at Valley Forge, the sponsor along with Woodmen of the World Insurance Society. Woodmen executive, Mark Theisen, also presented remarks.

Photo: John Fettig

Omaha and Nebraska have always been supportive of our military and veterans. Here, former Omaha mayor Bob Cunningham and I have laid out Patriot Awards that we would deliver to Omaha area businesses, professional offices, and public safety agencies. The Nebraska Employer Support of the Guard and Reserve (ESGR) sponsors the awards. Cunningham and I served for a number of years as co-chairmen of the committee in Omaha.

I took these photos more than a decade ago at Forest Lawn Cemetery during the American Legion Memorial Day service. This cemetery, established in 1885, is Omaha's largest, with excellent landscape design that conveys a sense of peace and tranquility. Hard-surfaced roads provide easy access to all sections to accommodate its visitors. Beginning with the Civil War, veterans of World War I and II, as well as the Korean and Vietnam wars, are buried here. The American Legion Post No. 1 honors them annually for their service to our country. For more than 25 years, this group has presented a patriotic program concluding with a 21-Gun salute and Taps on Memorial Day.

Military Chaplains Colonel Frank Lordemann and Major General William J. Dendinger, United States Air Force Ret. On October 15, 2005, Col. Lordemann received the Legion of Merit during his retirement ceremony held at Offutt Air Force Base. Major General Dendinger presented the award to Col. Lordemann at the base's Chapel and congratulated him on his many achievements during more than a quarter of a century serving his country. His legacy lives on in the Chaplain Corps.

After his ordination to priesthood in 1972, while serving Sacred Heart parish from 1972 to 1977, Fr. Lordemann sought counsel from a priest from the Archdiocese of Omaha who was serving as Cadet Wing Chaplain at the U.S. Air Force Academy Colorado Springs — Chaplain William J. Dendinger. Following Chaplain Dendinger's advice, Fr. Lordemann visited with Archbishop Daniel E. Sheehan about his desire to serve as a U.S. Air Force chaplain. Archbishop Sheehan granted his request, and Fr. Lordemann realized his dream of serving as a chaplain.

Later, Chaplain Dendinger would be promoted to Major General and appointed as the Chief of the Air Force Chaplain Service in Washington, D.C. He retired in 2001 and returned to the Archdiocese of Omaha to serve as pastor of St. Stephen the Martyr. He was ordained Bishop of the Diocese of Grand Island on December 13, 2004. Bishop Dendinger currently resides at the Cathedral of the Nativity of the Blessed Virgin Mary in Grand Island.

Fort Rosecrans National Cemetery, in Point Loma, California, overlooks San Diego and the bay. It is named after William Starke Rosecrans, a Union general in the Civil War. It became a National Cemetery on October 5, 1934. Recently, the addition of concrete walls for cremated remains replaced the former chain link fencing. This change made it possible for thousands of World War II veterans to be interred there. Prior to that time, the cemetery had been closed for new burials.

IN MEMORY OF
WILLIAM
EUGENE
ROARTY
NEBRASKA
ARM3
USNR
WORLD WAR II
OCTOBER 17 1924
MARCH 7 1945
PH

The gravesite of William Eugene Roarty is special to our family. Roarty, a North Platte native, was lost at sea while serving as Navy airman in the Pacific during World War II. His remains were never found. His parents were my uncle and aunt, Bill and Marian Roarty. The marker at Fort McPherson is among dozens of servicemen and women missing in action.

Photographer unknown

It was a historic day in our city in 1973 when a South Omaha street was named for a Korean War hero, Edward "Babe" Gomez. He had served with the First Marine Division in Korea and was awarded the Medal of Honor, posthumously, for his valor in saving the lives of fellow Marines.

Pictured at Gomez Avenue are, from left: Mayor Ed Zorinsky (later a U.S. Senator); an unidentified Marine Corps officer; Mr. and Mrs. Modesto Gomez, Babe's parents; Ray Stavneak, World War II Marine veteran; Bill Ramsey, presenting a First Marine Division plaque to Mrs. Gomez for the family; former mayor Gene Leahy, a Korean War Veteran, helped make the memorial avenue possible.

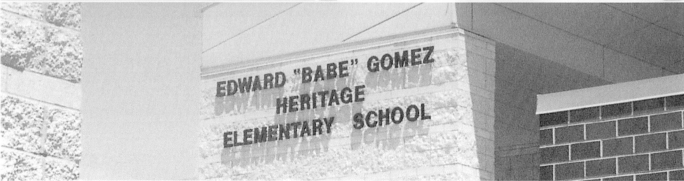

During World War II, United Service Organization (USO) opened centers across America to provide entertainment for servicemen and women. As troop trains raced across the country, one unlikely stop in the Midwest became famous as the North Platte Canteen. This city of 12,000 hosted more than six million GIs beginning in December 1941. Until the Canteen officially closed in 1946, the people of North Platte continued to give a warm welcome to those who had served their country so bravely and were now on their way home after achieving victory on all fronts.

Members of the armed forces came through North Platte daily during the war years. The Union Pacific Railroad main line through the city provided a pathway for people and products for decades. Overnight, these same tracks bore innumerable troop trains as well as machinery and supplies for the defense of the country. Once North Platte's passenger deport, the Canteen was transformed into a hospitality center as residents organized teams to greet troops during their brief stop — typically as short as 10 minutes. Beginning on Christmas Day 1941, the servicemen were amazed as they heard total strangers speak words of genuine welcome and express sincere gratitude to them for defending their land. Generous men, women and children waved wholeheartedly, then smiled warmly as they handed out hot coffee, baskets of food, and treats.

For the war's duration, the ritual began at 5 a.m., continued through the day into the evening, and ended sometime after midnight when the last troop train pulled away. People in surrounding cities, towns, and states joined the effort. Although food was rationed, somehow the contributing families found a way to provide hearty and homemade sandwiches, fruit, cakes, and cookies.

NORTH PLATTE CANTEEN

Photo: Nebraska State Historical Society

Another civic leader and business executive, Robert Daugherty, received a recognition from the First Marine Division Association. Daugherty served in the Marine Corps in World War II and was chairman of Valley Manufacturing (later Valmont Industries) in Valley, Nebraska. He was a generous booster of the Corps and the community. From left: Barney Zielinski, Bill Ramsey, Daugherty, and Bill Blum.

This photograph details the General Crook House Museum, located at 5730 North 30th Street in Omaha. The building, constructed in 1879, is on the grounds of Fort Omaha, known originally at Sherman Barracks and then Omaha Barracks.

General George Crook, a Civil War and National Indian Wars hero, eventually became a defender of Native American rights. Although he was named as a defendant in the 1879 trial of Standing Bear v. Crook, it is believed that General Crook helped to arrange the trial for Ponca Chief Standing Bear. A historic statement was made when Judge Elmer Dundy determined that American Indians were persons within the meaning of the law. It was also established that the Ponca had been illegally detained when they left Indian Territory in January 1879.

Built in an Italianate style, the Crook House is an example of the "no-nonsense grandeur" of the military frontier. The 1880s Victorian Period is evident in the interior furnishings of the museum; starting in early November, the Crook House Guild assists area designers and design students in transforming each room in the house as they may have looked during the holiday seasons of the 19th century.

The authentically restored home of General Crook is on the National Register of Historic Places.

Mrs. Clifton "Anne" Batchelder was the grande dame of Republican politics in Nebraska for decades. She was also a patriot and a Red Cross canteen driver in Europe in World War II. Her future husband was a decorated Army colonel when they met in Germany. Robynn Tysver took this photo during a parade celebration for Victory '95. The parade, in downtown Omaha, was one of numerous special events marking America's and the Allies' victory in World War II. Valmont's chairman, Bob Daugherty, was honorary chairman at the event. Ed Birchfield, a retired Air Force colonel and director of corporate relations for Valmont, directed the organization of the amazing event.

This significant memorial is located just north of the Omaha-Douglas Civic Center plaza. The metal plaque was dedicated on May 28, 1975, with city and country officials in attendance. It was my privilege to serve as master of ceremonies for the event. I was representing the First Marine Division Association, a sponsor of the small but impressive and important tribute.

There was some question at the time whether Bob Kerrey enlisted in the Navy in Lancaster or Douglas County. After the plaque was completed, it was later decided his name should have been on the memorial. There is now a separate plaque honoring him; it sits directly below the original plaque.

PLACED BY
American GI Forum - *J.J. Juarez*
Marine Corps League - *M.R. Wuerth*
1st Marine Division Association - *W.E. Ramsey*
Omaha/Douglas County Building Commission - *J.J. Cavanaugh*

In 1995, officials dedicated a Korean War Veterans Memorial in Washington, D.C., not far from the Vietnam Memorial and the Lincoln Monument. Two messages inscribed in silver on black marble summarize the essence of the war: "Freedom is Not Free" and "Our nation honors her sons and daughters who answered the call to defend a country they never knew and a people they never met."

Korean War Monument. Another view of the Korean War Veterans' Memorial.

Our Nation Honors Her Sons And Daughters Who Answered The Call To Defend A Country They Never Knew And A People They Never Met
1950 - KOREA - 1953

This is a close-up photo of a Korean War warrior sculpture at the Korean War Memorial in the nation's capital.

It was a sentimental and patriotic time in the nation's capital as we celebrated the long-awaited Korean War Veterans Memorial dedication in July 1995. Pat and I were with Jim and JoAnn Mortensen to honor those who served our country. The inscription on the memorial reads:

OUR NATION HONORS HER SONS AND DAUGHTERS WHO ANSWERED THE CALL TO DEFEND A COUNTRY THEY NEVER KNEW AND A PEOPLE THEY NEVER MET.

1950 - KOREA - 1953

As my buddy Jim Mortensen and I passed in review along with Korean and Vietnam veterans, with the Joint Chiefs of Staff looking on, we recalled: We were "Freedom Fighters," as the South Korean war memorials describe us. Is there a better title anyone could ask for? Thanks, America, for remembering.

Remember the hills and mountains of Korea,
And the blood, the dust, and the snow and the rain.
And remember our buddies always,
So they shall not have died there — in vain.
                                        -Richard Marshall

I am at WOW Radio-TV — my first job after graduating from Creighton University — getting the latest information from the Associated Press news wire.

THE ASSOCIATED PRESS

Photo: Bob Mockler, WOW Radio-TV

Breaking News

Newsman Ramsey with my trusty Bell & Howell movie camera on the Platte River Bridge between Omaha and Lincoln during a winter flood in the 1950s. I was lucky I wasn't blown into the icy river rushing by that night.

Photo: Radio & WOWT News Man

Nebraska and surrounding states were scared to a standstill in February 1958 as Charles Starkweather, a young man from Lincoln, embarked on a murder spree. Starkweather's 14-year-old girlfriend, Caril Ann Fugate, accompanied her beau on a killing journey across the Great Plains. In the end, 11 men and women were brutally slain.

Authorities eventually captured Starkweather near Douglas, Wyoming, after a car chase. This photo shows the murder weapons — a revolver and knife — laying on a table atop a copy of the *Rocky Mountain News*. The headline shouted "Mad Killer Captured." Starkweather was tried and executed in the electric chair at the Nebraska State Penitentiary in Lincoln in 1959.

Grave marker of Charles Starkweather in Wyuka Cemetery.

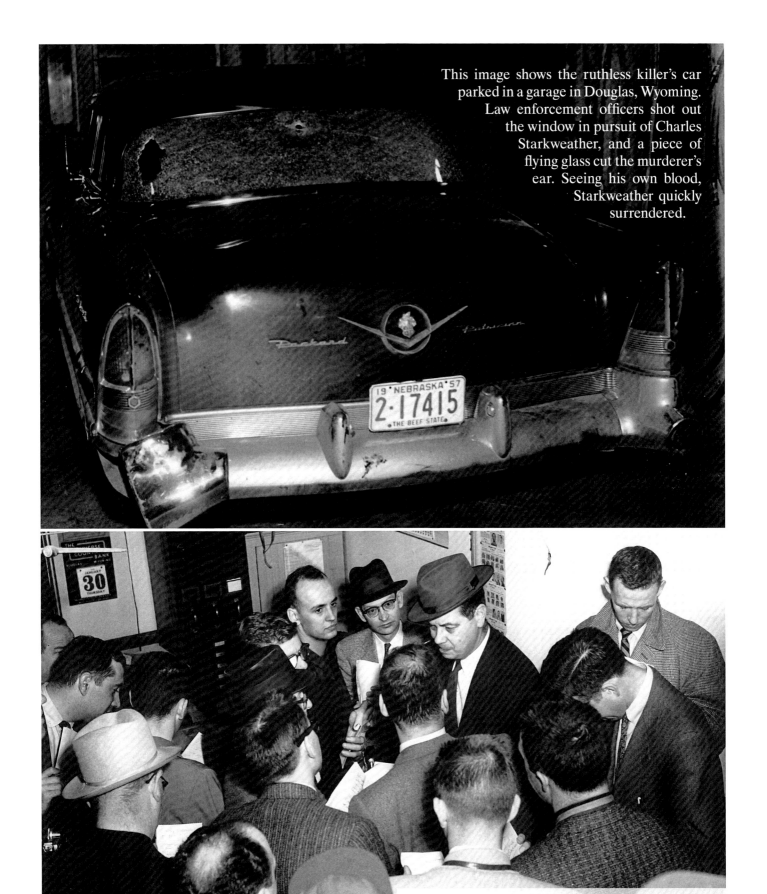

This image shows the ruthless killer's car parked in a garage in Douglas, Wyoming. Law enforcement officers shot out the window in pursuit of Charles Starkweather, and a piece of flying glass cut the murderer's ear. Seeing his own blood, Starkweather quickly surrendered.

Reporters and newsmen gathered to learn the latest developments in the Charles Starkweather murder spree. I am at far right taking notes in the Douglas, Wyoming, Sheriff's office.

The Gilmore Home destroyed by fire

A heartbreaking assignment for a young reporter, I took this photo when covering the tragic Gilmore nursing home fire at 501 Frank Street in Council Bluffs, on February 13, 1957. The blaze destroyed the home and killed 17 residents; many more were injured in the fast moving inferno. Rescuers — police and fire personnel, medical professionals, and volunteers — joined in the effort to aid the injured and transport the dead to mortuaries. It was one of the city's most deadly fires. A new fire detection system had just been installed at the nursing home, but it wasn't clear whether or not it was functioning at the time of the fire. There was no sprinkler system.

Mayor James Mulqueen and Mayor Glenn Cunningham view the now-controlled Missouri River 40 years after the memorable flood of 1952. The two mayors proved to be perfect team leaders in defeating the marauding Missouri.

Photo: Omaha World-Herald

This unique marker is located at the Dodge Riverside Golf Club. Wilson Custom Design Tile Company created the tribute and used the design of their artist, Beth Davis, who has completed more than 16 historic tiles for the City of Council Bluffs. The plaque reads:

IN HONOR OF ALL WHO WORKED TO SAVE THE CITIES OF COUNCIL BLUFFS AND OMAHA FROM THE HISTORIC MISSOURI RIVER FLOOD OF APRIL 1952 — LED BY JAMES F. MULQUEEN, MAYOR OF COUNCIL BLUFFS GLENN CUNNINGHAM, MAYOR OF OMAHA WITH 50 YEARS OF GRATITUDE FROM THE CITY OF COUNCIL BLUFFS — IOWA WEST FOUNDATION, APRIL 25, 2002

To Gene Ramsey — Best Wishes — Ray "Sugar" Robinson

Pound for pound, the greatest boxer of them all, Sugar Ray Robinson. This star welterweight and middleweight was one of my heroes, both during childhood and still today. This is an autographed photo sent to me as a youngster; Eugene, "Gene," is my middle name, and the name I was called while growing up.

I received one of my most cherished childhood gifts when I got to sit ringside with Dr. Neil Danberg and watch Robinson box one of Omaha's favorite prizefighters, Art Hernandez. The decision — a draw. Hernandez may have out-pointed the champ, but I was happy. It was a memorable match.

Luckily, I got to see Sugar Ray fight in Omaha at the City Auditorium in the 1960s at the end of his career. Even then, as a 41-year-old, he drew in a bout with his 23-year-old opponent. He was a great fighter and human being.

This photo of the Texas School Book Depository clearly shows an assassin's comparatively easy shots that took President John F. Kennedy's life in Dallas on November 23, 1963.

Lee Harvey Oswald's position at the sixth floor window in the building where he was employed meant the fatal bullet was fired at approximately 88 yards, probably less, and with scope on the 6.5 mm caliber Carcano rifle. Rifle ranges at most military bases have 100-300 and 500-yard targets with no scope in standing, sitting, and prone positions.

I also visited Parkland Hospital where the mortally wounded president was taken. There I saw the doorway where the president entered and even the trauma room where he expired. I was asked not to take pictures and I certainly obliged. President Kennedy joined the ranks of many heroes who died serving their country — a U.S. Navy hero and a martyr for the United States. God bless his sacrifices.

This picture was taken on a happy occasion — a victory dinner celebrating another successful year for the United Way of the Midlands. Charles "Chuck" Peebler, a top executive of Bozell & Jacobs advertising and public relations firm, was the United Way campaign chairman. He spoke about the importance of the mission of United Way: to utilize the caring power of people who live and work in Douglas and Sarpy Counties in Nebraska and Pottawattamie County in Southwest Iowa, connecting people in need with its services.

The theme of this evening was simply "Thank You." The event was held at one of the city's most popular venues, the Fontenelle Hotel Ballroom. Noted architect Thomas Rogers Kimball designed the building in the Late Gothic Revival style. Built in 1914, the structure was demolished in 1983.

Omaha is blessed with one of the most versatile and talented artists. Jim Horan, longtime Omaha *World-Herald* artist, is shown with a special comics feature he created to promote the 1970s "Return to the River" campaign. "Return to the River" paved the way for our the city's riverfront revitalization during the 21st century.

Mayor Gene Leahy advanced the idea and formed a volunteer citizens committee to begin the planning. Leahy and others asked Mike Yanney, an executive at Omaha National Bank, to chair the group. It was my assignment, from both Leahy and Yanney, to formulate the public relations strategy. It remains one of the highlights of my career in PR.

One PR idea was to contact the *World-Herald* executives to learn if they would consider a comic section to reach youth and all fans of the funnies. The *World-Herald* agreed and assigned Horan to create the one-time Sunday comic strip.

His first assignment was to take the proof to the mayor for his approval. Horan admitted it seemed a formidable job to meet the mayor by himself. He entered the office and displayed the new addition to the comics. Horan said the mayor instantly raced around the desk and kept yelling, "It's perfect; it's great!" "I was shocked," Horan said, "and relieved." Sure sounds like the Gene Leahy I knew dating back to our heading off to the Korean War as young Marines.

"Captain Riverfront" received rave reviews and the interest in the exciting project continued to grow. Later, I took a naval-type captain's cover to Jim's office at the newspaper and took this photo of him proudly holding the comic strip. A short time later, a story of the promotion appeared in the *Editor & Publisher* magazine, the Bible of the newspaper industry.

Horan is retired but continues doing aviation illustrations for national clients. He has also completed approximately 120 caricatures for the Omaha Press Club "Faces on the Floor" ceremony. I salute "Captain Riverfront," Mayor Gene Leahy, Mike Yanney, and our team — affectionately called the River Rats.

Photo: City of Omaha

Who will ever forget the crushing ice that devastated our area in October 1997? Even Halloween was cancelled due to nature's harrowing trick. The official snowfall measured nine inches; the icy avalanche toppled trees, power lines, and even some structures.

What wasn't affected was the spirit of midlanders who somehow returned the battered communities to normalcy. Days without power in homes and businesses were depressing and posed what seemed an insurmountable challenge.

Our home and business office were darkened for eight days — many others longer than that. Nebraska National Guard members and armies of volunteers banded together, along with public service and safety and security officials, to restore order after two weeks in crisis.

Mayor Hal Daub joined this team of city employees and National Guardsmen to help clear a street. The mayor and other civic and social leaders showed the fighting spirit of Nebraska and Iowa. It was surely the worst of times and the best of times. To all who helped, thank you.

Promoting Education

I was greatly influenced by one of my teachers. She had a zeal not so much for perfection as for steady betterment — she demanded not excellence so much as integrity.

— Edward R. Murrow

Sunday **Magazine of the**
MIDLANDS®
The Omaha World-Herald / June 2, 1968

I was asked to do a cover shot for Creighton University's annual report while working in public relations at my alma mater from 1965 to 1970. I took this sunset shot at the top of the long stairway behind St. John's Church on the Creighton campus. These two seniors accommodated my foibles of having the sun "just right" before shooting the picture. The photo said, "Into the Future," to me. Later the photo was selected by editor Hollis Limprecht for the cover of the Omaha *World-Herald Sunday Magazine of the Midlands.*

Graduation: '68
What Now?
Page 5

Central High School has been a landmark in Omaha since the mid-1800s. It was Omaha's first all-grades public school, opening in 1859. Ten years later, the Nebraska Legislature donated the old capitol building at 21st Street and Capitol Avenue for use as a high school. After being declared unsafe, the building was demolished in 1870 and a new high school building was constructed and opened a year later.

The original Central High building, made of red brick, faced east. Its main structure included north and south wings with a 150-foot-tall tower that dominated the downtown area. It was named Omaha High School and became a tourist attraction. In 1911, President William Howard Taft paid a visit to the school and was eager to climb the tower for a panoramic view of the city.

By 1897, overcrowding and lack of proper ventilation prompted the school board to approve a larger building. The cornerstone for the current Central High was laid in November 1900. Built in stages, the east side of the school was built first and classrooms from the old building were used for the duration.

John Latenser, Sr., architect, designed the building using the late 19th and 20th Century Revivals style. Twenty years later, the grounds needed attention due to the steep incline of Dodge Street. While the grading took place, Dodge was closed for a year. Central was left with a 20-foot drop until a new terrace and flights of stairs eliminated the problem and provided students with an attractive campus to this present day.

CENTRAL HIGH SCHOOL

Johnny Carson's sidekick and second banana, Ed McMahon, was a vital part of the "Tonight Show" for so many years. Bob Reilly, an Omaha PR icon, was a high school classmate of McMahon's in Massachusetts. They became fast friends and Reilly was the Godfather for one of the McMahons' children.

Ed was a Marine Corps pilot in World War II and Korea. I met him in New York at a Marine Corps luncheon in the 1970s. Here I caught him on the run at the Hilton Hotel in Omaha to present him with a Marine Corps award from the First Marine Division Association of Omaha. Can't we all still hear Ed introducing Johnny... "Heeeerrrrreeeessss Johnny!"

University of Nebraska football coach Tom Osborne and I had been discussing a public relations project unrelated to the university. I took the opportunity to photograph this highly regarded coach and mentor.

He and his wife, Nancy, established the TeamMates Mentoring Program, which helps young people in need. Coach Osborne returned to the university as its athletic director in 2007.

DR. JEANNE PRICKETT

Dr. Jeanne Prickett, superintendent of the Iowa School for the Deaf, stands in front of the high school entrance of the 155-year-old institution. It is located in Council Bluffs, on Harry Langdon Boulevard. Langdon was a leading comedian in the silent movie era and a Council Bluffs native.

Dr. Prickett succeeded longtime superintendent Dr. William P. Johnson as the leader of this famed school, which has for more than a century prepared students from Iowa and Nebraska for their futures. Most recently, Dr. Prickett headed a capital campaign to raise funds for a state-of-the-art science center. Community and area volunteers and benefactors helped reach the campaign goal, along with Paul J. Strawhecker, Inc., development counsel.

Gary Lee Price created the bronze sculpture, "Story Time," in the background. A boy and girl sit on giant books as they study. In 1991, Price was elected a member of the National Sculpture Society. His theme is "Lifting the Human Spirit Through Sculpture." Thousands of his sculptures may be seen in public and private collections throughout the world.

Valuing Religious Men and Women

While there yet remains one dark soul without the light of God,
I'll fight — I'll fight to the very end.

— *General William Booth* Founder of the Salvation Army

Following the liturgy for Archbishop Daniel E. Sheehan at Saint Cecilia's Cathedral on October 30, 2000, the funeral procession arrived at Calvary Cemetery. The Fourth Degree Knights of Columbus formed an honor guard allowing the procession to proceed to the cemetery altar.

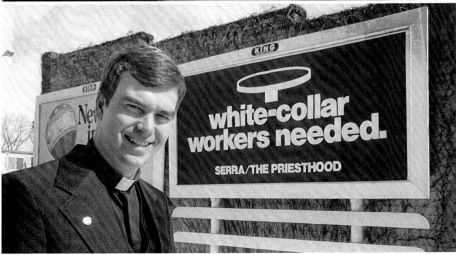

The Rev. Jim Kramper stands near a Serra promotional billboard. Fr. Kramper was chaplain of the Serra Club of Omaha from 1972 to 1981. He braved 20-degree temperatures and snowdrifts to pose for this photo. The theme became part of the Serra national and international outreach to promote vocations to the priesthood and religious life.

Mother Teresa was a warmly welcomed overnight guest at the Monastery of the Poor Clare Sisters. She paid a visit to the chapel before the Sisters escorted her to the monastery's library, where a comfortable chair awaited her. Mother Teresa surprised the Abbess, Sister Mary Clare, when she directed her to sit there while the guest of honor seated herself on one of the wooden, straight-backed library chairs.

Mother Teresa was establishing a new branch of the Missionaries of Charity in Guatemala and entrusted their foundation to the prayers of the Poor Clare Sisters in Omaha. It was her practice to ask a contemplative order to pray for the successful mission of each newly established convent. Sister Mary Clare said that when Mother Teresa retired for the night, the sisters never knew if she slept in the bed or prayed throughout the night. She had no suitcase but rather traveled with a carryall that resembled a bucket.

As she prepared to leave the Poor Clares, Mother Teresa paused with the sisters in front of the monastery just long enough for me to take this photograph.

This photo features the Rev. Robert P. Hupp, executive director of Boys Town, with Mother Teresa of Calcutta, India. Mother Teresa and her companion, Elizabeth Collins, made a welcomed stop in Omaha to receive the Father Flanagan Award for Service to Youth in May 1976. Fr. Hupp took Mother Teresa on a tour of the campus, during which she met some of the citizens of Boys Town and their teachers. This is one of the few photographs in which the greatly admired missionary nun was smiling.

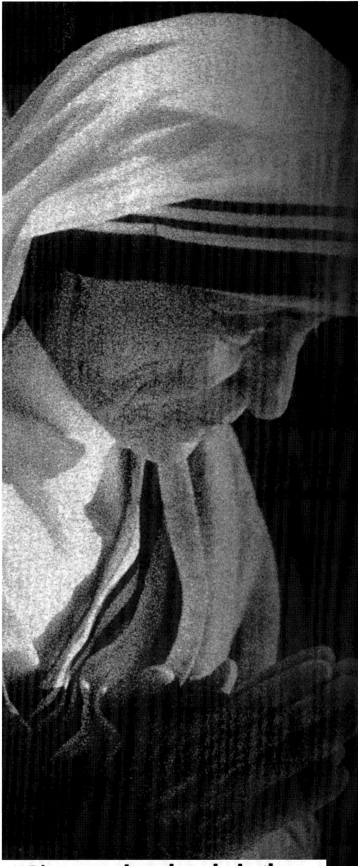

"Give your hands to help them and your heart to love them."

Mother Teresa of Calcutta
at Boys Town, May, 1976

This photo was taken as Mother Teresa led the group in the opening prayer at Omaha's old Hilton Hotel award luncheon. I was the public relations director at Boys Town when Fr. Hupp asked me to provide transportation for our guest of honor during her time here. I had the privilege of meeting Mother Teresa and her companion at the airport and escorting them to all their stops throughout her visit to our city. As I bade her goodbye almost 40 hours after I had met her, I knew my life had been changed forever. She had made a lasting impression for good. I picked up an early afternoon Omaha *World-Herald* for her. She put it into her little satchel, thanked me for my friendship, gripped my hand with her arthritic, gnarled hand, and told me to keep up the wonderful work I was doing. She turned, walked away, turned again and waved.

A LIVING SAINT!

The Hilton luncheon was classic. A packed ballroom watched and listened in awe to our distinguished visitor. She stepped onto a small riser, just barely visible over the lectern. But her words need no riser. In 12 short minutes, she inspired the crowd with her love and zeal.

And when the luncheon ended, Mother Teresa had a most unusual request of me. "Bill, could I take the candles with me?" We had lovely candelabras on the tables and the candles were burned throughout the luncheon. I said, "But, Mother Teresa, the candles are half burned." She replied, "Yes but they're half good." My secretary, Mary Lou Koterzina, and I quickly gathered the candles for her and put them in sacks supplied by the hotel.

In the meantime, she had told Fr. Hupp she needed a monstrance for her new convent in Guatemala. Fr. Hupp said he had one back at Boys Town. After the lunch, I walked to the door with Fr. Hupp and Mother Teresa and watched them as they boarded his 4-wheel-drive Toyota and headed west to pick up the monstrance. I was a bit concerned since she had a mid-afternoon flight to catch, and we also had promised a stop at the Sisters of the Cross convent. Upon their return from Boys Town, we rushed Mother Teresa and her companion to the convent with little time to spare for the impending flight.

Clarence Walker, Mayor-elect of Boys Town, presented honorary citizenship to Mother Teresa during the well-attended award luncheon ceremony held at the downtown Hilton Hotel. Before Mother Teresa proceeded to Eppley Airfield where she boarded a jet, she visited the Good Shepherd Sisters, another cloistered community in Omaha.

This is the last formal photograph of Archbishop Daniel E. Sheehan. On June 11, 2000, the archbishop presided at the 7:30 a.m. liturgy for the St. Vincent de Paul Society at Our Lady of Lourdes Church in Omaha. That afternoon, the Rev. Patrick Harrison drove him to join Bishop Fabian Bruskewitz and five bishops for the confirmation of more than 1,500 children in Lincoln at Pershing Auditorium. The next day, Archbishop Sheehan left for the Mayo Clinic in Rochester, Minnesota, with longtime friends Dr. John and Kimmy Hartigan. By the end of the week, the diagnosis was confirmed: the archbishop had an inoperable cancerous brain tumor. They all returned to Omaha, where the archbishop was admitted to Alegent Bergan Mercy Hospital. He was later admitted to Mercy Care, where he died on October 24, 2000.

On October 30, Saint Cecilia Cathedral quickly filled with designated representatives from the more than 150 parishes of the Archdiocese of Omaha and from various religious organizations, family members, and members of the clergy. His final resting place is on the west side of the altar at Calvary Cemetery. The sepulchral monuments bear the names of the bishops and archbishops who have served the Archdiocese of Omaha.

Richard Cardinal Cushing of Boston made a surprise visit to Duchesne College and Academy of the Sacred Heart during an Omaha meeting. His Eminence was most cordial during his brief stay; dozens of Religious of the Sacred Heart were in a heavenly state in the presence of one of the most famous international leaders of the Catholic Church. With my Speed Graphic shaking, I am surprised that the picture of our honored guest wasn't a blur. Prayer brought this photo into focus.

The Boys Town water tower identifies the incorporated village in Nebraska where the former Father Flanagan's Boys' Home national headquarters is located. The mission of the non-profit organization is to care for children and families across the country.

The Rev. Edward J. Flanagan, a priest of the Archdiocese of Omaha, founded the boys' orphanage in 1917 and soon learned that his downtown facilities were inadequate. By 1921, Fr. Flanagan established a site 10 miles west of Omaha named Boys Town, where one of its "citizens" was elected mayor. Other facilities on campus soon followed, as the ever-growing community gradually expanded to include schools, chapels, cottages, police and fire departments, a post office, and a large gymnasium. The community was an ideal place where young boys and men, between 10 and 16, received an education qualifying them for higher education. Many learned a trade to train them for future employment.

In 1985, Archbishop Daniel E. Sheehan appointed the Rev. Val J. Peter, an archdiocesan priest and a longtime theology professor at Creighton University, as the fourth director of Boys Town. An energetic, bright and innovative priest, Fr. Peter continued to build on Boys Town's strengths and introduced new programs to better address the children of the 1980s, who were experiencing an even broader range of difficulties.

Under Fr. Peter's dynamic direction, Boys Town established 13 satellite facilities across the country. Married couples that are charged with training six to eight children staff these homes. The couples, known as family teachers, are professionally trained.

The Rev. Val J. Peter, the fourth executive director Boys Town. He served as the director from 1985 to 2005. During his tenure, Boys Town expanded its influence to 15 states and the District of Columbia. A longtime professor at Creighton University, Fr. Peter's vision for the future of this internationally known center for youth brought numerous new programs and expansion to its home campus. He often said, "I am the keeper of Father Flanagan's dreams."

This photo depicts Mother Connie Campbell, RSCJ, president of Duchesne College in the 1960s, saying her evening prayers as she walked around the campus grounds at Duchesne Academy and College in Omaha. She was well liked by all who knew her.

Sculptor Eugene Kormendi created this statue of Msgr. Flanagan with four of his boys in 1948. The monument is centrally located on the grounds of Boys Town, Nebraska. The memorial plaque on its base reads as follows:

1886 – 1948
IN MEMORY OF RT. REV. MONSIGNOR
EDWARD J. FLANAGAN
FOUNDER OF BOYS TOWN AND
RECIPIENT OF VARIETY CLUBS FIRST
HUMANITARIAN AWARD

HIS DICTUM:
"THERE IS NO SUCH THING
AS A BAD BOY."

ERECTED BY THE
VARIETY CLUBS INTERNATIONAL
1948

Kormendi was a sculptor of religious statuary. Born in Budapest, Hungary, Kormendi immigrated to the United States and was on the faculty and a sculptor in residence at Notre Dame.

His wife, Elizabeth Kormendi, was a sculptor and painter whose specialty was ceramics. In 1947, Msgr. Flanagan wrote a letter of thanks to her for creating the magnificent aluminum Stations of the Cross for the Dowd Memorial Chapel.

The monument in Calvary Cemetery features St. John Vianney located in the section for priests of the Archdiocese of Omaha. Pope Benedict XVI declared a "Year for Priests" beginning in June 2009. Ross and Josephine Lorello, longtime Omaha residents, commissioned the lifelike sculpture by Dale Lamphier. They hoped to pay tribute to the many dedicated priests with this image of St. John Vianney, who is known as the patron of parish priests and was later designated the patron for all priests.

ST. JOHN VIANNEY
PATRON OF PARISH PRIESTS
DEDICATED MAY 26, 1997

EVERY DAY IS A GIFT
EACH PRIEST
A GIFT FROM GOD
ROSS AND JOSEPHINE
LORELLO

I took this photograph July 10, 2010, when more than 175 seminarians from archdioceses and dioceses throughout the United States were in Omaha for a 10-week summer session offered by the Institute for Priestly Formation (IPF) at Creighton University. IPF Founders are: the Rev. George A. Aschenbrenner, S.J., the Rev. Richard J. Gabuzda, the Rev. John P. Horn, S.J., and Kathleen Kanavy. They were joined by seminarians and women religious from various countries working at Boys Town during the summer months at the invitation of the Rev. Val J. Peter, former executive director, and the Rev. Steven E. Boes, executive director of Boys Town and pastor of Immaculate Conception Church (Dowd Chapel). The seminarians and their instructors were touring the campus of Boys Town learning about its founder, Father Edward J. Flanagan. The Serra Clubs of Omaha have sponsored this event since 2001.

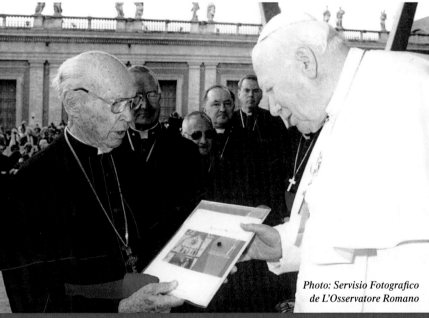

Photo: Servisio Fotografico de L'Osservatore Romano

This photo features the Rev. Michael Mukasa of Uganda, a summer visitor to St. Margaret Mary parish. He was in residence for a time and also continued his college studies in this country. Later, Fr. Mukasa assisted at St. Wenceslaus parish in Omaha, where his close friend and pastor, the Rev. Mel Merwald resided. The school children at both parishes loved Fr. Mike. He is shown here in front of St. Margaret Mary Church. He was a popular teacher at both schools and a fine role model for our youth.

Archbishop Daniel E. Sheehan traveled with the Archdiocesan Pilgrimage from Omaha to Rome in the spring of 2000. While there, he waited his turn in line to personally greet the Holy Father. He asked the pontiff's secretary to deliver for him "A Gentle Shepherd," his biography written by Betty Dineen Shrier and me. The gracious monsignor suggested that Archbishop Sheehan should present it directly to Pope John Paul II. The moment he placed it in the hands of the Holy Father, a photographer snapped the photograph to capture this historic scene on April 5, 2000. Upon his return to Omaha, Archbishop Sheehan shared this story with us and gave us the original photograph. We were overwhelmed with surprise and gratitude. Few authors see their work so dramatically conveyed.

From left: Kathy Kanavy, Archbishop Curtiss, Rev. Richard J. Gabuzda, Rev. John Horn, S.J.

A historic advance in the growth of the Institute for Priestly Formation occurred in March 2008. The Most Reverend Elden Francis Curtiss, Archbishop of Omaha, signed a decree recognizing the Institute for Priestly Formation as a Public Association of the Faithful in the Archdiocese of Omaha.

A Public Association of the Faithful is an officially recognized body in the Church which receives a mission from the Church to achieve the purposes of its charism.

The Most Rev. George J. Lucas, Archbishop of Omaha, is standing in the studio following his broadcast of an inspiring spiritual message at the Spirit Catholic Radio Network in Omaha. In the past year, Spirit Catholic Radio has reached more than one million people in eastern and central Nebraska and western Iowa. The radio network has been serving its listening audience for more than a decade, and continues to extend its signal strength across Nebraska.

Photo: Ervin Photography

The Rev. John P. Schlegel, S.J., has been a man of action during this past decade as president of Creighton University. The hard hat he is wearing in this photo aboard a bulldozer is symbolic of his exceptional leadership as an administrator, accomplished diplomatic skills, and tireless efforts as a civic leader.

Creighton University announced in July 2010 that Fr. Schlegel would retire the following July. This prompted many to examine his lengthy list of accomplishments. His fundraising efforts have resulted in remarkable success; enrollment has increased significantly and the university has received repeated national recognition for high academic standards and initiatives raising the bar for excellence in learning.

His concern for the wider community led to diversity outreach and students' participation in assisting the homeless. The school established health clinics, as well, further affirming Fr. Schlegel's belief that an urban campus should be strongly connected to its community. Shortly after becoming president, he said, "It is absolutely essential, in my opinion, that an urban university not be an ivory tower. It would be ideal not to have walls and have the entire city as the campus."

CONSTRUCTION COMPLETED DURING FR. SCHLEGEL'S ADMINISTRATION:

Hixson-Lied Science Building
Wayne and Eileen Ryan Athletic Center
D.J. Sokol Arena
Mike and Josie Harper Center for
Student Life and Learning

The summer of 2010 witnessed a reason to celebrate with a special family. The Rev. Stephen E. Boes, executive director of Boys Town, stands with his parents, Gene and Mary Jane Boes of Elgin, Nebraska, on the occasion of his 25th anniversary of priesthood in the Archdiocese of Omaha. They are in front of Immaculate Conception Church (Dowd Chapel), where Fr. Boes had presided at a Mass for family and friends who gathered at Boys Town to offer congratulations.

Prior to his duties at Boys Town, Fr. Boes served as the Mission Director at St. Augustine Indian Mission in Winnebago, Nebraska.

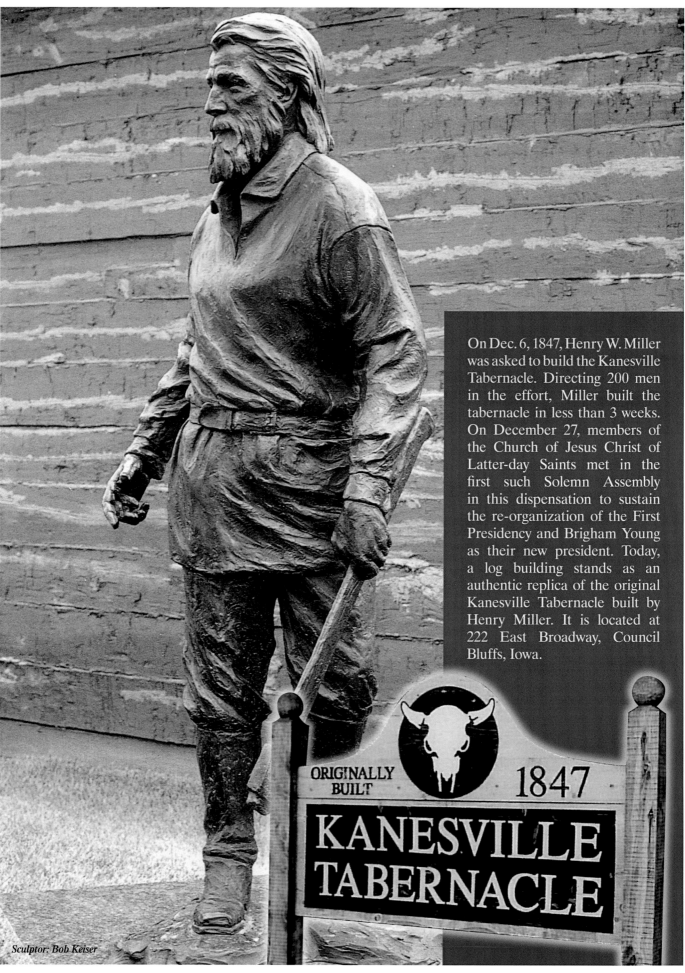

On Dec. 6, 1847, Henry W. Miller was asked to build the Kanesville Tabernacle. Directing 200 men in the effort, Miller built the tabernacle in less than 3 weeks. On December 27, members of the Church of Jesus Christ of Latter-day Saints met in the first such Solemn Assembly in this dispensation to sustain the re-organization of the First Presidency and Brigham Young as their new president. Today, a log building stands as an authentic replica of the original Kanesville Tabernacle built by Henry Miller. It is located at 222 East Broadway, Council Bluffs, Iowa.

ORIGINALLY BUILT 1847

KANESVILLE TABERNACLE

Sculptor: Bob Keiser

Photo: From left: Bill Ramsey; J. D. Anderson, president of Guarantee Mutual Life and event chairman; and honoree, Rose Blumkin.

The inaugural Free Enterprise Person of the Year Award went to Rose Blumkin, aka "Mrs. B," founder of the Nebraska Furniture Mart, during an event that occurred in 1979. I was president of the Rotary Club of Omaha at the time and had initiated the award, along with fellow Rotarian and Omaha businessman, Rufus Amis. The Rev. Carl M. Reinert, S.J., longtime president of Creighton University and a close friend of Mrs. B, was the event's speaker. It was a dramatic and enjoyable day.

THE COLONELS HICKAM JOIN THE FAMOUS SALVATION ARMY BRASS BAND DURING OMAHA'S INCLEMENT WINTER AND FEISTY SPRING WEATHER LAST YEAR.

COL. MILFORD (LEE) HICKAM, COMMANDER OF THE WESTERN DIVISION OF THE SALVATION ARMY, ADDED HIS NOTES AT A GOOD FRIDAY PRAYER SERVICE AT THE GENE LEAHY MALL IN OMAHA. IT WAS A DREARY, BITING COLD NOON HOUR.

COL. PAT HICKAM BRAVED 10 DEGREE WIND CHILL AT THE ARMY'S ANNUAL TREE OF LIGHT'S CHRISTMAS EVE REPORT AT THE HALL OF JUSTICE LAWN AT 17TH AND FARNAM, AND IN SPITE OF THE WEATHER, BOTH PLAYERS PERFORMED WITH SKILL AND GUSTO.

THE HICKAMS ARE ON THEIR SECOND TOUR OF DUTY IN THE WESTERN DIVISION. PRIOR TO THEIR RETURN, THEY HELPED LEAD THE SALVATION ARMY BACK INTO RUSSIA, SERVING IN THE MOSCOW AREA.

1996 Campaign

Pope Pius IX dedicated this statue of St. Peter on Easter Sunday in 1847. The previous pope had commissioned sculptor Giuseppe De Fabris to create this impressive figure.

In his right hand St. Peter is holding the keys to the kingdom, symbolic of the power bestowed on him by Christ. His left hand holds the scroll bearing the words, "ET TIBI DABO CLAVES REGNI CAELORUM," which translates in *The New Jerusalem Bible* to, "I will give you the keys of the Kingdom of Heaven…"

I photographed this historic statue during my trip to Rome for the Serra International meetings in 2003.

Honoring Houses of Worship

I never weary of great churches. It is my favorite kind of mountain scenery. Mankind was never so happily inspired as when it made a cathedral.

—Robert Louis Stevenson

Our Savior's Lutheran Church was established in Milford, Nebraska, in the late 1800s. Its origins were in Staplehurst, Nebraska. The Milford church held services until 45 years ago. Drivers can glimpse this picturesque scene as they travel I-80. We admire the dedication of those who founded and maintained this lovely house of worship still standing amid the tall prairie grass. Passers-by might call this "The Lonely Church on I-80."

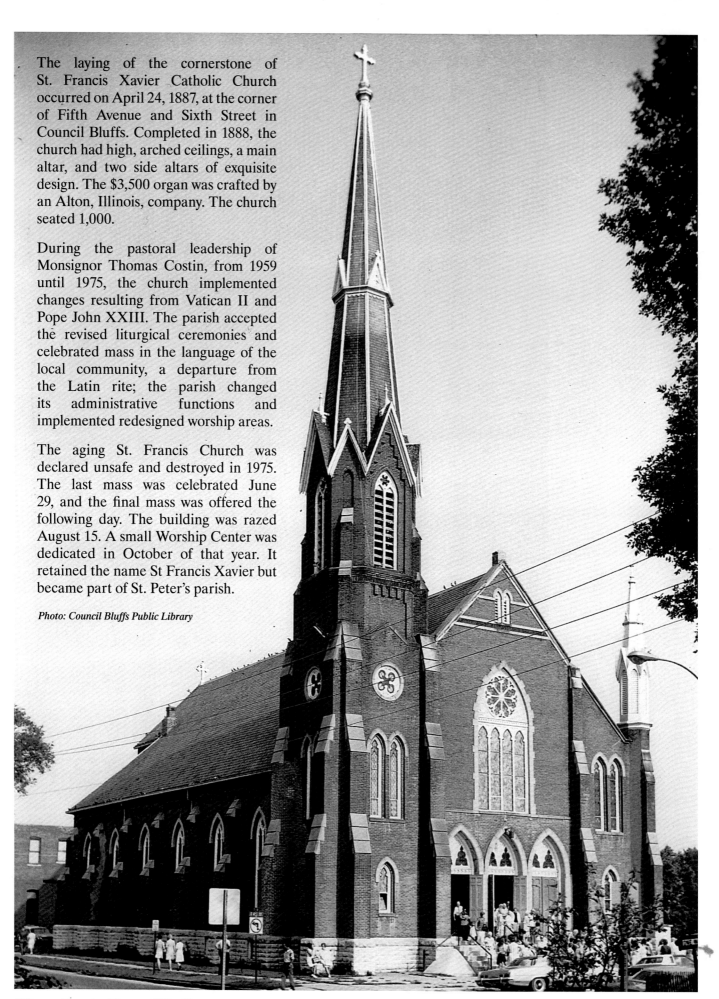

The laying of the cornerstone of St. Francis Xavier Catholic Church occurred on April 24, 1887, at the corner of Fifth Avenue and Sixth Street in Council Bluffs. Completed in 1888, the church had high, arched ceilings, a main altar, and two side altars of exquisite design. The $3,500 organ was crafted by an Alton, Illinois, company. The church seated 1,000.

During the pastoral leadership of Monsignor Thomas Costin, from 1959 until 1975, the church implemented changes resulting from Vatican II and Pope John XXIII. The parish accepted the revised liturgical ceremonies and celebrated mass in the language of the local community, a departure from the Latin rite; the parish changed its administrative functions and implemented redesigned worship areas.

The aging St. Francis Church was declared unsafe and destroyed in 1975. The last mass was celebrated June 29, and the final mass was offered the following day. The building was razed August 15. A small Worship Center was dedicated in October of that year. It retained the name St Francis Xavier but became part of St. Peter's parish.

Photo: Council Bluffs Public Library

TED SELDIN

Theodore "Ted" Seldin, chairman of the Seldin Company, holds a photograph I took several years ago when he gave me a tour of Omaha's Temple Israel. Seldin presented the framed picture as a gift to Rabbi Aryeh Azriel, the chief rabbi for the Temple since 1988. Before coming to Omaha, Rabbi Azriel had served as a rabbi in Baltimore, Maryland. The Temple had been in previous locations in Omaha before the congregation bought land at 69th and Cass streets in 1951. The building seats 300 in its sanctuary and 500 in the social hall, and features 11 classrooms and a kitchen to accommodate the congregation. The new building's symbols reflect its mission: "tikkum olan," or "Repairing the world."

Seldin, a Council Bluffs native, is a member of the Temple's congregation and serves as an advisor to Rabbi Azriel. Ted had been an active duty Air Force lawyer for two years in 1957 when he joined the family real estate firm that his father founded in 1923. Today, the Seldin Company owns and manages thousands of apartments and more than 1.25 million square feet of mixed-use retail and office space in five Midwestern states.

In 2010, the Greater Omaha Chamber of Commerce inducted Seldin into the Omaha Business Hall of Fame. The Chamber cited his example of managing affordable housing for seniors; his firm built and manages 1,000 apartment units for these citizens under HUD's Section 8 assistance program. A board member of the National Association of Home Builders, he also helped craft national legislation for low- and moderate-income family housing.

Seldin was recognized for bringing a thriving retail area to the now-called Benson Park Plaza at 72nd and Ames streets. The Seldin Company also donated land as well as infrastructure there valued at $1.8 million to be used as the new headquarters for Goodwill Industries.

Located in the scenic Platte River Valley, the Holy Family Shrine at 23132 Pflug Road in Gretna attracts more than 20,000 visitors a year from throughout the world. Those driving east or west on a stretch of Nebraska's Interstate 80 cannot resist looking at the unusual chapel perched on a high hill amid its peaceful 23-acre site.

Travelers of all religious persuasions are welcome to stop here for a time of reflection and relaxation as they enjoy colorful gardens and stone paths that surround the chapel and the visitor's center.

The arching wood frame of the chapel's façade, 49 feet tall, speaks to the viewer of grain waving in the fields, with wheat representing our source for bread. That sight, upon reflection, is an image of the bread of life — the Eucharist.

The front of the chapel bears an etching in a pane of glass 16 feet tall. The image is of Jesus, Mary, and Joseph — the Holy Family. The water flowing through the limestone floor represents the Holy Spirit as it courses its way from the entry along the sides of the pews. The 12 wooden structures arching across the chapel remind us of the 12 apostles. Those who visit the Holy Family Shrine leave feeling enriched and blessed for the time spent there.

St. Cecilia Cathedral, designed by noted architect Thomas Rogers Kimball in 1905, was considered among the ten largest cathedrals in America upon completion in 1959. Located at 701 North 40th Street, this eminent structure is one of Omaha's most significant buildings for its unmatched architecture and beauty. This revered edifice, in the Spanish Renaissance Revival style, is listed on the National Register of Historic Places and is a designated Omaha Landmark. St. Cecilia Cathedral is the cathedral church of the Roman Catholic Archdiocese of Omaha.

The photo shows a member of the Pope's Swiss Guard on duty at the Vatican. I took this picture in 2003, during the Serra International board meeting in Rome. I was serving as the president of the USA Council of Serra International at the time. My wife and I enjoyed touring the numerous historic and religious sites in Rome and the surrounding areas.

I despise all adjectives that try to describe people as liberal or conservative, rightist or leftist, as long as they stay in the useful part of the road.

—Dwight D. Eisenhower

Harry S. Truman, President of the United States from 1945 to 1953, was a keynote speaker for Creighton University's Alpha Sigma Nu gathering at the Joslyn Museum in 1961. He gave a very brief talk and then fielded questions. All of his answers were short and somewhat salty, mixed with a few "hells" and "damns." Later at a reception at the late Tom and Marge Walsh's home at 92nd Street and West Dodge Road, I was taking photos for the university. I had my Speed Graphic press camera. Midway through the reception, one of the flash bulbs exploded. The entire party came to a screeching silent stop. President Truman broke the spell, saying, "I thought for a minute, those damn communists were shooting at me again." We breathed a sigh of relief, especially this red-faced photographer. I shot this picture of President Truman with the Walsh daughters that day, as well as one of him and the youngest girl at the piano, playing none other than the "Missouri Waltz."

Hubert H. Humphrey, the 38th Vice President of the United States, was the principal speaker at the annual Brotherhood Dinner at Peony Park Ballroom in Omaha in the late 1960s. I was a member of the NCCJ (National Conference of Christians and Jews) board and unofficial photographer for the organization. It was my privilege to shoot this picture as the vice president delivered a memorable address. Muriel, his wife, can be seen at the right of the lectern. The vice president was a congenial fellow and seemed pleased to have been invited to the sellout event.

Later that night, it was reported that a man with a rifle was apprehended on the rooftop of the motel where the vice president was registered. It was noted that he was never in any danger.

The vice president also spoke at Creighton University in the spring of 1968, the presidential election year. Humphrey would be the Democratic candidate that fall. My secretary, Leonore, and I thought it would be appropriate to present Mrs. Humphrey a bouquet as she accompanied him to Omaha on his campaign swing. We carefully placed the box under a front row chair.

As the Secret Service agents "swept the room" one last time, they were shocked to spot the flower box. They asked me what was in the box and I replied, "Yellow roses for Mrs. Humphrey." With that information, they opened the box and spread the roses on the floor. They quickly returned them to the box, which we then presented to our special guest.

Rev. Harry Linn, S.J., Creighton University president, shown escorting presidential hopeful Senator Eugene McCarthy of Minnesota, around campus in the spring of 1968. It was one of five such tours for our distinguished political leaders and presidential candidates that election year.

President Richard Nixon's death in the spring of 1994 reminded me of his visit to Creighton University when I was director of public relations. I took this photo of Nixon as he was leaving the campus that December day in 1967. He was a practicing attorney at the time and was beginning his 1968 campaign effort in earnest. The Creighton visit prompted other political candidates to make sure Creighton was on their itinerary. Others who spoke on campus in the spring of 1968 included Vice President Hubert Humphrey, Gene McCarthy, Harold Stassen, and Robert Kennedy.

New York Senator Robert F. Kennedy, addressing Creighton University students in front of the Brandeis Student Center. It was a warm afternoon, and Senator Kennedy placed his suit coat on the railing of the steps nearby. People jammed the quadrangle to listen to his talk, which the national media widely quoted. This photo, one of my personal favorites, was used in several publications.

The tie bar he wore that day depicted a gold PT-109. When I told him I was a fan of his brother, President John F. Kennedy, Senator Kennedy took the tie bar off and handed it to me. He said, "You should have this." I have worn it on special occasions ever since that day. This and other photos of the senator were taken in mid-May 1968, just weeks before Sirhan Bishara Sirhan assassinated the presidential candidate in a Los Angeles hotel.

Navy Lt. John F. Kennedy was commander on Navy boat PT-109 during World War II in the Pacific Theater. The vessel was cut in two after being rammed by a Japanese destroyer, *Amagiri*, off the Solomon Islands on August 2,1943. Seamen Andrew Kirksey and Harold Marney were lost, two other crew members were severely injured, and their craft was gravely damaged.

With only the forward hull afloat in surrounding flaming waters, Kennedy relied on his experience as a varsity swim team member and used a life jacket strap clenched between his teeth to tow his enlisted machinist mate, who was badly burned. The men made their way during the 4-hour swim to the deserted Plum Pudding Island. The small island provided no food or water, so Kennedy swam about 4 kilometers to Olasana Island. He then returned to his men and led them to this haven filled with coconut trees and water. After six days, the PT-157 rescued the men when they learned from scouts the location of the survivors.

JOHN F. KENNEDY

PHOTOGRAPHED BY DAVE HAMER, AUGUST 1959

I made this photograph of John Kennedy at a backyard barbeque at the home of Bernard Boyle, an Omaha attorney and chairman of the Nebraska Democratic Party. Mr. Kennedy was sampling support for his 1960 successful run for the presidency. It was a warm summer afternoon and the atmosphere was relaxed as the media gathered around for a brief news conference. The sun was filtered by overhanging trees, which created finely diffused lighting. Of the dozen exposures I made this was the best.

–*Dave Hamer*

After viewing this amazing picture, you undoubtedly understand my reason for asking Dave Hamer to be the photo editor of this book.

–*Bill Ramsey*

This photograph of President Gerald Ford was in the press kit given to the media prior to the NEBRASKAland Foundation Statehood banquet honoring President Ford in 1988. Ford represents a striking portrait of a World War II Navy veteran, congressman, and U.S. President.

Photo: NEBRASKAland Foundation staffer

I arranged for this historic photo to be taken at the annual NEBRASKAland Foundation Statehood banquet at the Capitol in Lincoln in 1988. The recipient of the Distinguished NEBRASKAlander Award was former President of the United States, and Nebraska native, Gerald Ford. Also adding to the history was the inclusion of Nebraska's first and only woman governor, Kay Orr. I was president of the NEBRASKAland Foundation, the sponsor of the annual event. The photo was taken in the Governor's Mansion prior to the dinner.

Omaha businessman, community leader, and volunteer James Paxson led the effort to create a park near Ford's birth site to honor the former president.

Governor Kay A. Orr, then the first Republican woman in the United Sates to be elected governor of Nebraska, performed with her husband, William "Bill" Orr at an annual Omaha Press Club Ball in the late 1980s. During this fundraising show for journalism scholarships, "First Gentleman" Bill Orr graciously accepted being teased about that moniker. Nebraska had never elected a woman as governor until 1986.

Born in Burlington, Iowa, Kay A. Stark attended the University of Iowa. She moved with her family to Lincoln, Nebraska, in 1963, and began volunteering as a Republican Party worker. Filling a midterm vacancy, Kay Orr was appointed as treasurer in 1981. She was elected to that office in 1982 and served in that capacity until 1986, when she was elected governor of Nebraska.

Council Bluffs Mayor Thomas P. Hanafan, a lifelong resident of the western Iowa city, holds the record for mayoral longevity. His fellow City Council members elected him to serve as mayor in 1985. In 1988, he was elected to a full term when the job became a full time commitment. He continues in that capacity to this day. Mayor Hanafan is a committed and active participant in many efforts throughout the community, including the United Way of the Midlands, the Metropolitan Area Planning Agency, the Iowa West Racing Association, and the Rotary Club. He is past president and board member for the League of Iowa Municipalities, as well.

This affable and energetic city leader appears to thrive on his whirlwind schedule. It's hardly an official meeting if the mayor isn't in attendance, someone once said. That may be true. And his love of his hometown comes through loud and clear as he strives to make Council Bluffs the finest community in southwest Iowa and in the entire state.

His other activities include being a sports official for high school basketball (retired), and football (currently 38 years). He has coached football, basketball, soccer, baseball, and softball.

He is a dreamer, but he is also a doer. His dynamic attitude and visionary leadership have helped Council Bluffs reach heights never imagined a few decades ago. Mayor Hanafan brings people together, delegates responsibility, and trusts that these individuals will complete their tasks.

One of Nebraska's great political leaders both as governor and as U.S. senator, J. James Exon was also a good friend and humanitarian. Still visible on this signed photo is Senator Exon's hand-written message: "To my friend and favorite photographer, Bill Ramsey." I was working with him and my good friend, Bob Reilly, during Exon's successful campaign for U.S. Senator.

I photographed colorful Omaha Mayor Gene Leahy in his office at the interim City Hall, in a building formerly known as the Elk Building. Leahy served as mayor from 1967 to 1973. Earlier, Leahy had served as a municipal judge after earning his law degree at Creighton University. A Korean War Marine Corps veteran, he and I trained together at Camp Pendleton, California, and sailed on the same troop ship to Korea in March 1951.

Mayor Gene Leahy is standing by the entrance to the Gene Leahy Mall in Omaha. Also known as Central Park Mall, and located at 13th and Farnam streets, the mall has pathways around a large lagoon, two waterfalls, and gigantic slides that children as well as their parents enjoy. Various musicians offer outdoor concerts in the mall during the summer months, and during the winter holiday season the trees sparkle with the glow of thousands of holiday lights.

Leahy, a Marine Corps veteran of the Korean War, had been a deputy county attorney and a municipal judge before his election as mayor of Omaha. His belief in the advantages of riverfront development was among the reasons for this mall bearing his name. It proved to be a catalyst in the renovation of an area in the city that had deteriorated over the years. When the Omaha Press Club honored him as its first "Face on the Barroom Floor," artist Jim Horan's image pictured Leahy in a bunny suit that he wore as a costume to promote the Easter Seals Agency. The mayor also read the Omaha *World-Herald* Sunday comics to children on a weekly television program wearing an admiral's hat he also wore in some parades. This hat is included in the drawing at the Press Club that was presented on November 1, 1971. Horan said, "He was a fun-loving person who took the 'honor' with good nature."

When the University of Nebraska-Omaha announced it wanted to cut football from its athletic department, he became a champion to retain the popular sport. The Gene Leahy Mall, a major impetus for downtown redevelopment, is now regarded as a thriving commercial, residential, and cultural center in this city.

SEEING DOUBLE

Leland Terry and his son, longtime congressman Lee Terry, following a Memorial Day ceremony at Memorial Park in Omaha. The senior Lee and I worked for a time as newsmen at WOW in the late 1950s.

Two Nebraska Senators led a Memorial Day weekend ceremony in 1997. From the left: Chuck Hagel and Bob Kerrey, both Vietnam War heroes. I snapped this photo during a rain-swept news conference at Memorial Park. The event included a 4-day display of the Traveling Vietnam Memorial Wall and a rededication of the Korean-Vietnam Peace Memorial. I headed a committee that raised funds to build the monument. Completed in 1976, it was restored, and the monument area enhanced, thanks to Vietnam Veterans Omaha Chapter 279, headed by Bill Henry and Dave Ciaccio, the landscape architect who did the plantings at the monument. The statue is being lifted off its base behind the senators, as work begins to transport it for refurbishing.

In 1974, Vice President Gerald R. Ford was welcomed as a guest at the Omaha Press Club. The vice president was making a visit to his hometown, where he was born in 1913. He was the club's first recipient of the "Good News Award" and gained the title of honorary member. Ford was vice president from 1973 to 1974, when he was elected President of the United States and remained in office until 1977.

From left: Vice President Gerald R. Ford; Howard Silber, president of the Omaha Press Club; and Bill Ramsey, then public relations director at Boys Town and president-elect of the Omaha Press Club.

Vice President Spiro Agnew attended the first anniversary of the Omaha Press Club in June 1972. Agnew served as the 39th Vice President of the United States from 1969 to 1973. He was honored with the "Face on the Barroom Floor." Later, the club's south room was named "The Spiro Agnew Conference Room." That all changed when he resigned as President Richard Nixon's vice president.

This photo was taken at a gathering of the past presidents of the Omaha Press Club celebrating the 25th anniversary of the club in 1996.

Photo: Kurt A. Keeler

Back row ascending, from left: the late Frank Scott, Voice of America staffer and well-known local broadcaster. He also served for a time as the OPC executive director; Pat Hall, veteran Omaha *World-Herald* photographer; Dave Hamer, acclaimed photojournalist at several television stations, past president of the National Press Photographers, and photo editor of this book; Terry Forsberg, television news reporter and executive with American Gramaphone Records; Jim Clemon, longtime *World-Herald* reporter and editor; Cheri Griffin, aka Alex Kava (best-selling author of mystery novels), past KETV television reporter; David A. Haberman, professor emeritus of Journalism and Mass Communication at Creighton University; James Denney, veteran Omaha *World-Herald* reporter/photographer; Howard Silber, longtime Military Affairs writer for the Omaha *World-Herald*; Barry Combes, former director of public relations, Union Pacific Railroad; Steve Murphy, news director at WOW-TV.

Lower front row, left to right: Dottie Sater (white sweater), WOW-TV reporter; Julie Zelenka, writer at WOW-TV and the Omaha *World-Herald*; Mary McGrath, Omaha *World-Herald* reporter; Joe McCartney, former director of public relations, Union Pacific Railroad and past WOW-TV reporter/photographer and Journalism faculty member at the University of Nebraska-Omaha; Joni Baillon (Mrs. Vern Wood), KMTV personality.

At the center of the rail: Bill Ramsey, former WOW-WOW-TV newsman and photographer, author and public relations professional; Chris Christen Nelson, then president of the club and Omaha *World-Herald* writer.

From left (seated): Archbishop Bergan, Leo A. Daly, A.F. Jacobson, Sid Cates. From left (standing): Peter Kiewit, John H. Becker, Monsignor Nicholas Wegner.

This event, featuring some of our community's leading citizens meeting at the Chancery of the Archdiocese of Omaha with The Most Reverend Gerald T. Bergan, offered me another rare privilege as a photographer. I took this photo circa the late 1960s or early 1970s. Archbishop Bergan died July 12, 1972.

Three well-know Omaha leaders at a Catholic Church event at Aksarben Coliseum during the 1960s. Archbishop Gerald T. Bergan at the lectern, joined on stage by V. J. Skutt, chairman of Mutual of Omaha (left), and Monsignor Daniel E. Sheehan, future archbishop of Omaha.

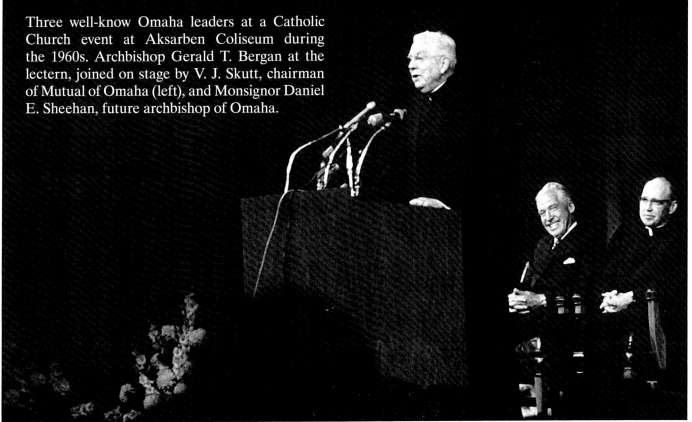

Two important community leaders and I were present at an awards ceremony at Peony Park. I took on the duty of "plaque carrier" at this memorable event. Interim Mayor Bernie Simon is presenting the 1987 Mayor's Partnership Award to Michael H. Walsh, chairman and CEO of the Union Pacific Railroad, for his and the railroad's outstanding contributions to the community. Walsh also served as chairman of the Greater Omaha Chamber of Commerce in 1990.

A milestone day for Bill Ramsey Associates, Inc., happened in 1999 when we received the Greater Omaha Chamber of Commerce Golden Spike Award. Chamber board member, John Gottschalk, longtime president of the Omaha *World-Herald*, was on hand to congratulate a shocked recipient. The citation read: "For outstanding contributions to the stability and future growth and development of the Greater Omaha Community." As a former Union Pacific employee, and knowing that my mother had retired from the railroad, the award had a special meaning

CHARLES DURHAM

Charles "Chuck" Durham was one of the most honored philanthropists in Omaha. Chuck and his wife, Margre, reached out to a vast number of educational, humanitarian, and medical causes in Nebraska and Iowa.

Chuck Durham served as an engineering consultant to Omaha and Council Bluffs during the catastrophic threat of the Flood of 1952. I took this photo of Durham as he recalled those daunting days gazing across the Missouri River from the shore of Council Bluffs. Among his many key decisions at that time was to summon the Vicksburg, Mississippi, "Flood Fighters," as he called them.

There was an urgent need for heavy equipment, and Council Bluffs officials turned to Durham and the Henningson Engineering Company in Omaha, which would later be known internationally as Henningson, Durham & Richardson, or HDR.

Durham had worked in the city during the late 1940s, rebuilding the community's infrastructure. When Mayor James Mulqueen asked Durham if he could secure the additional sandbags and flashboards, which would be critical to saving the city, Durham replied, "I don't know if it's possible, but we're going to try like hell."

Durham scoured the Midwest and turned up more than 100 pieces of equipment to help strengthen the main levees. The victory over the ominous threat brought the two cities together as never before. Later he traveled extensively, hoping to persuade communities to avail themselves of federal subsidies for infrastructure improvements. HDR became the premier regional planner of sewer and other city development projects.

It was my privilege to join nine other area writers in producing a memorable biography of Chuck, and, of course, Margre. The volume is entitled "Lucky." The courage, generosity, and compassion of this giant community advocate are warmly chronicled in the book.

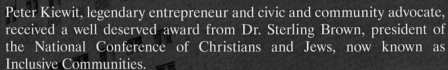

Peter Kiewit, legendary entrepreneur and civic and community advocate, received a well deserved award from Dr. Sterling Brown, president of the National Conference of Christians and Jews, now known as Inclusive Communities.

The Kiewit Corporation was known as Kiewit Brothers when it was founded by his father, also named Peter Kiewit, in 1884. When his father died, Peter Kiewit headed the firm from 1924 until his death in 1979. His accomplishments during that time were impressive. Peter Kiewit Sons' Incorporated expanded to become one of the largest construction organizations in the world. His far-reaching vision also led him to become an active participant in the Omaha area and nationally.

To keep the Omaha *World-Herald* locally owned, Kiewit bought the newspaper in 1963. In 1964, Walter Scott, Jr., was elected to the board of Peter Kiewit Sons' Incorporated, and in 1974 he became president of the board. Later that same year, Peter Kiewit died and Scott succeeded him as chairman. Under the terms of Peter Kiewit's will, the employees bought the newspaper in 1979.

Scott's leadership brought the Kiewit Corporation through new challenges and opportunities. The company constructed a nation-wide fiber optic network that spun off as Level 3 Communications. The company, which headquarters its corporate office at 35th and Farnam streets in Omaha, is employee-owned and subdivided in regional companies that are further subdivided into geographical districts. Holding a reputation for honesty and integrity has earned the Kiewit Corporation the respect and goodwill of the worldwide community.

Louis Finocchiaro, Sr., in his warehouse. When 16-year-old Louis Finocchiaro, Sr., his 19-year-old brother, Vincenzo, and an uncle, Giuseppe, left Sicily for America in 1914, they had no idea how their lives would change. Friends who had gone before them advised that Omaha was a good destination.

Young Louis was soon on the streets of downtown Omaha singing the first three words of English he learned: "Bee, News, Herald." He was thrilled when he got a job washing dishes at a restaurant at 12th and Douglas streets. By 1917, he and Vincenzo started a cheese factory in Bennington. But when Vincenzo was drafted into World War I that year, Louis' heart was broken.

Following several other jobs, he and Vincenzo had saved their money to send to their parents in Sicily. In addition to the wholesale company in 1920, the brothers soon had a chain of six groceries in Omaha named Finocchiaro Brothers. He said, "We were pleased with our early success and life in Omaha became a real joy when my mother and sister, Rosa, came to America." Life in America was good for the Italian immigrants and St. Philomena parish became the heart of "Little Italy."

Louis married Mary Raneri in 1928. The two would raise three sons, Vincent, Jerry, and Louis, Jr.

Finocchiaro and his sons: from left, Louis, Jr., Louis, Sr., and Vincent in front of their building. The family's wine company has become famous in the Midlands. Vincent and Louis became the second-generation leaders of Finocchiaro Enterprises.

At 81 years old, Louis Finocchiaro still went to work every day in the office pondering the ledgers, writing orders, and mingling with the staff. When asked if he had a formula for success, he replied that he just had his own philosophy: "Love your roots, your family; try to get along with people; get a good education, that's a key; develop a sense of responsibility; be self-sufficient, and work hard." Then he reflected, "It's been a good life; thank God, my family, and my country for it."

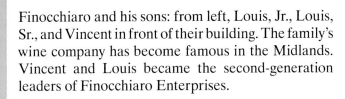

A well-deserved recognition for a dedicated business leader and community philanthropist. Ted Seldin, chairman of the board of Seldin Company, is inducted into the Greater Omaha Chamber of Commerce Business Hall of Fame in April 2010. David G. Brown, president and CEO of the chamber, presented Seldin with an impressive medallion as part of the tribute.

Seldin and his company is my oldest continuous business client, dating back more than 25 years. Our advertising and public relations firm marked its 30th anniversary in 2010. It has been a wonderful combination of friendship and business over the years.

John Mulhall, Irish immigrant, founder of Mulhall's Nursery. Omaha has been blessed with a vibrant and productive Irish population since its early years. Mulhall is one of those latter-day Irish immigrants.

This son of Erin has put down deep roots in his adopted land and has made his entrepreneurial mark by helping people grow plants and trees in America. It was my privilege to introduce Mulhall as the recipient of the Rotary Club of Omaha Free Enterprise Award in 1997. The award luncheon was in mid-March and proved to be an early St. Patrick's gift for this caring, giving, and talented lad from the "Old Sod."

Mulhall's Nursery started modestly in the family's garage at 51st and Fort streets in 1956, and has grown to be one of the largest nurseries in the Midlands. Mulhall said of coming to America, "He did the best he could with what he had, and that wasn't much." He began as a gardener in Ireland and went on to become chairman of the board in America — and only in America.

A historical turning point in Council Bluffs occurred in 1996 when Harveys Casino Hotel opened for business on the Missouri Riverfront. It also brought a native son back home. Verne Welch, an executive for Harveys at Lake Tahoe, was appointed General Manager of Harveys in the Bluffs.

Welch is a Council Bluffs native, an alumnus of Thomas Jefferson High School, and a Naval Intelligence officer. He has also become one of his hometown's leading volunteers for an array of charitable and civic causes.

In recent years, Harveys has become Harrah's Council Bluffs Casino & Hotel.

The H.H. "Red" and Ruth Nelson family has contributed significantly to Council Bluffs, Omaha, and the midlands. Both senior Nelsons are deceased, but their legacy lives on in the good works and business acumen of the John P. Nelson family. John is chairman and CEO of SilverStone Group, and a former King of Aksarben. He and his wife, Anne, have been honored by many organizations for their philanthropy and volunteer commitments.

The next generation is John H. Nelson, president of SilverStone Group, pictured here with his grandfather on the occasion of Red Nelson's recognition by the Rotary Club of Omaha to honor him with its Free Enterprise Award.

OMAHA'S FAMOUS

From Left: Bill Noyes, a leader in public safety, Dan Gordman and Mayor A.V. Sorensen, attending the opening of the Gordmans store in the 1970s.

Photo: Duchesne College Staffer

This photo was taken on Commencement Day at Duchesne College in the early 1960s. I was director of public relations for the school at the time, one of the finest experiences of my life. On this day, I received an honorary degree from the college.

From left: Mrs. Paul "Rachel" Gallagher, community volunteer extraordinaire; John "Jack" Shonsey, bank executive and chairman of the Duchesne capital campaign in the 1960s; Bill Ramsey; and Lloyd Skinner, chairman and president of Skinner Macaroni Company and philanthropist who received the first Blessed Philipine Duchesne Missionary Award for his support of missionaries.

Nebraska's mythical Navy reached a high water mark on April 2, 1986, when two "real" Admirals attended the official launching of the Society of Nebraska Admirals at Freedom Park in Omaha.

Not only was the society born near April Fools' Day, by the way, but also the grand tradition of "Walking the Plank" made its first splash. John Hanlon, a charter officer of SONA (Society of Nebraska Admirals) got the idea as he was driving to the USS *Hazard*, a land-locked World War II minesweeper at Freedom Park. He knew there was no way to simulate walking the plank, so the ceremony, mercifully, consisted simply of the honorees walking the plank around the deck of the ship. The play on the old pirates' custom became an instant hit.

Coming aboard the USS *Hazard* first was Vice Admiral Ken Moranville, a native of Guide Rock, Nebraska, and then commander of the Navy's Third Fleet based in Hawaii, and Rear Admiral C.R. "Bob" Bell, then deputy director of the Joint Strategic Target Planning staff at Offutt Air Force Base.

Our first Fleet Commander of SONA was Frank Marsh, a longtime Nebraska political leader from Lincoln. I succeeded Marsh as the second Fleet Commander and have since been succeeded by retired Nebraska Air National Guard Brigadier Gen. Lloyd Johnson of Lincoln, along with many others.

The founding day also saw SONA members make this pledge: "To promote Nebraska's Good Life or walk the plank and drop into the depths of the dismal River." One of our state's most beautiful streams, I might add.

And they think politics is tedious! The introduction of this High Ropes course at the Omaha Home for Boys proved equally challenging to City Council members Ben Gray and Pete Festersen.

They were among a few good men and women whose tight rope experience helped them walk the heights. Outward Bound is a national non-profit education program that helps climbers defeat their fears. The two political leaders wisecracked their way over the swaying ropes, much to the delight of the grounded onlookers, as they supported the Omaha Home for Boys and its mission.

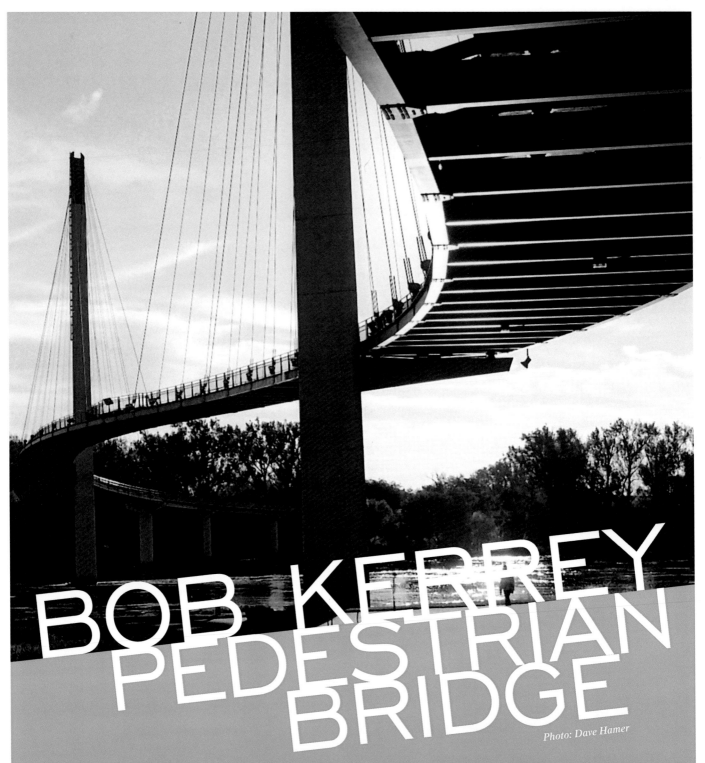

BOB KERREY PEDESTRIAN BRIDGE

Photo: Dave Hamer

This unique view of the Bob Kerrey Pedestrian Bridge is inviting. The bridge has become an icon of unity and friendship to cooperation between Nebraska and Iowa. More than 100 years ago the largest voluntary migration in the history of the world moved across the Missouri River in the Omaha and Council Bluffs area. These were the pioneers determined to settle the great American West.

The structure is the longest pedestrian bridge linking two states. Designed for walking and biking, the bridge has become a destination for residents and visitors who enjoy the 15-foot-wide walkway measuring 3,000 feet in length. On the Nebraska side, the 3-acre Omaha Plaza provides recreational activities. The Iowa landing is being constructed to provide a new River's Edge Park at the foot of the bridge. One of its features will be a 5-acre Great Lawn that will offer festivals, major events, and concerts that will draw Council Bluffs residents and visitors to the site.

Appreciating Pets and Animals

My favorite animal is the mule. He has a lot more horse sense than a horse. He knows when to stop eating. And he knows when to stop working.

—Harry S. Truman

When Mutual of Omaha's "Wild Kingdom" wanted its artist to create an original promotional image, the public relations department considered all options. Dave Hirsch, the artist at far right, is seeking a true print of the tiger's paw. With careful handling, the three zoo staff placed the animal's paw in ink and hoped his print would not smear as they coaxed the reluctant animal to place his foot on the paper below. This off-putting exercise did not sit well with the feline, whose threatening roar throughout the process seemed directed at the photographer.

One of the banks in Omaha selected this photo as an advertising promotion. Banks were known for giving gifts to their customers, and this fortunate canine eagerly awaited his dog biscuit as he sat behind the wheel at the drive-up teller window.

When the driver of M.J. Carriage Service spontaneously brought her horse to a halt at 18th and Harney streets, I could not resist capturing this unplanned photograph. Carriage rides have become an Old Market tradition adding to the lore and fascination associated with this historic and bustling community.

Indulging in the "Best of the Rest"

In every photographer there is something of a stroller.

— Henri Carter Bresson

William W. "Bill" Kratville, Union Pacific photographer in Omaha, seemed oblivious to what appears to be the approaching Union Pacific Railroad locomotive-train, "Big Boy," in the Council Bluffs rail yards. The giant locomotive is on display periodically in Council Bluffs and Omaha.

PEONY PARK

Joe Malec, Sr., owner of a restaurant and gas station on the Lincoln Highway in 1919, saw an opportunity looming when his neighbor, Carl Rosenfield, owner of Peony Gardens, had ever-increasing crowds stop at his 25 acres of peonies. Malec decided to add amusements to this roadside attraction at 78th and Cass streets in Omaha. In years to come, Joe Malec, Jr., would continue to add to the park's features for people of all ages to enjoy.

During the next 75 years, the 35-acre parcel would become a popular park that included a swimming pool complete with sandy beaches and waterslides. In addition, Malec built what would become known as the Royal Terrace Ballroom for dining and dancing. In the 1930s, the park became the Lawrence Welk Band headquarters, increasing its popularity. In later years, big name bands from the Swing Era played on a regular basis. Many still recall the charming Royal Grove, an open-air stage and orchestra shell with a white roof. The romantic dance floor area would accommodate 3,000 dancers.

In 1970, the park added amusement rides with a roller coaster, the "Seven Swings" ride, Wonderland, and the Galaxy roller coaster. In the open area west of the Royal Grove, the picnic and recreation grounds included a softball diamond. When my public relations firm was asked to compile a promotional brochure for Peony Park's 1990 summer season, the amusement park rides numbered 19, including the Ferris Wheel, Merry-Go-Round, a train, boats, and an umbrella ride. The combo pass included unlimited use of all rides, swimming pool, and waterslides — all for the price of $11.95.

People were disappointed to learn that Peony Park was put up for sale in 1993. Revenues had dwindled and the operating costs were becoming excessive. The land was sold to a commercial land developer who planned to turn it into a shopping center. The park officially closed after the 1994 summer season. Today the property contains the original Keno parlor, a bank and a grocery store, among other commercial developments. Throughout its existence, our citizens were proud of its status as Nebraska's largest amusement park and continue to recall with fondness the place where they once enjoyed "the time of their lives."

In 2001, Jim McGrath edited and compiled the book titled "Heartbeat: George Bush in His Own Words." He described a delightful story President George Herbert Walker Bush told at a fundraising breakfast for Governor Kay Orr at the Peony Park Ballroom on February 8, 1990. President Bush said, "I'm delighted to be here at this relatively early morning breakfast. It reminds me of the time I told our eldest grandson that the early bird gets the worm. He says, 'I think I'll sleep in and have pancakes.'" The banner behind the speakers' table read:

NEBRASKA AND GOVERNOR ORR
WELCOME PRESIDENT AND MRS. BUSH

Midtown Omaha is home to the headquarters of well-known corporations Mutual of Omaha, Berkshire Hathaway, and the Kiewit Corporation.

This part of the city includes several historic neighborhoods: Gifford Park, Joslyn Castle, Walnut Hill, Field Club, and the Country Club neighborhood. Homes dating from the 1880s can be found in the Hanscom Park neighborhood, which can be described as a vibrant, front-porch neighborhood.

Mutual of Omaha initiated a new neighborhood development in the area called Midtown Crossing at Turner Park. This vibrant community includes offices, apartments, condominiums, restaurants, a health club, and grocery store. Following Mutual of Omaha's upgrading and expansion of Turner Park, people are drawn to its spacious lawn, comfortable benches, and extensive tree-lined walkways. Thousands now gather there weekly for the annual "Jazz on the Green" summer concert series, formerly held at the Joslyn Art Museum.

This photo was taken looking toward the west on 30th Street between Dodge and Farnam.

The sign placed in this attractive landscaped area indicates the passerby is in the Leavenworth Neighborhood — Destination Midtown. It is located on the corner of 30th and Harney streets in Omaha.

A Coldstream Guard sentry was at rigid attention when I snapped this photo at the Royal Palace in May 1988. Her Majesty's Coldstream Regiment of Foot Guards, a regiment of the British Army, originated in Coldstream, Scotland, in 1650. I took this while on a vacation in London and Ireland. It is our all-time favorite vacation.

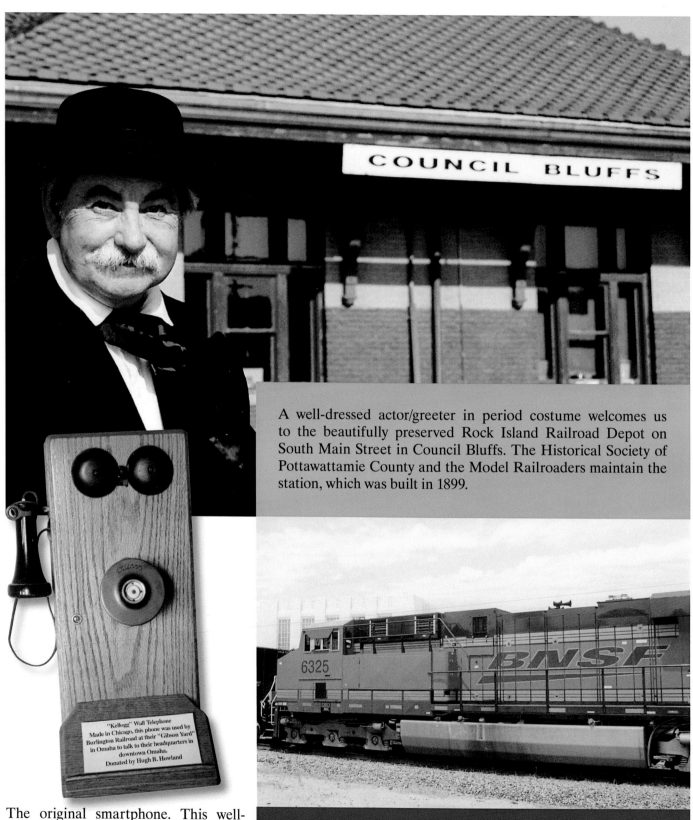

A well-dressed actor/greeter in period costume welcomes us to the beautifully preserved Rock Island Railroad Depot on South Main Street in Council Bluffs. The Historical Society of Pottawattamie County and the Model Railroaders maintain the station, which was built in 1899.

"Kellogg" Wall Telephone
Made in Chicago, this phone was used by Burlington Railroad at their "Gibson Yard" in Omaha to talk to their headquarters in downtown Omaha.
Donated by Hugh B. Howland

The original smartphone. This well-preserved telephone, on display at the Rock Island Depot in Council Bluffs, is a source of curiosity for younger visitors. The name "The Kellogg Wall Telephone" falls short of today's myriad varieties of phones. The Burlington Railroad used it in the "Gibson Yards" in Omaha.

I took this photo as an engineer guided the more than 70 freight cars over the Omaha tracks near the Amtrak National Rail Passenger Service terminal on South 9th Street. The BNSF logo identifies the Burlington Northern Santa Fe Railroad. Because my father was an engineer for Burlington Railroad for many years, I developed a deep respect and fascination for the railroads even as a youngster.

The Towboat "Omaha" nuzzles her barges under the Aksarben bridge across the Missouri River between Omaha and Council Bluffs. The barges are going to receive grain at Council Bluffs to be shipped downstream.

ABRAHAM LINCOLN

Abraham Lincoln came to Council Bluffs in 1859 to inspect a section of land on which he had made a loan. During his visit, he spoke with Grenville M. Dodge concerning the construction of a railroad to the Pacific.

From a wooded bluff they gazed across the broad Missouri River valley. Four years later, after Lincoln had become President of the United States, Council Bluffs was designated the eastern terminus of the first transcontinental railroad, and General Dodge was named its chief construction engineer. The Lincoln Monument at Oakland Avenue and Lafayette Avenue commemorates this visit.

Photo and description by
Council Bluffs Community Development Department

Epilogue

For Bill Ramsey, taking pictures was not a skill, but a passion.

— Tom Schmitt

Photo: *The Daily Nonpareil*

The word "epilogue" is defined as a piece of writing at the end of a work of literature or drama, used to bring closure to the work — and often to reveal the fates of the characters.

Not all books have an epilogue, but it is quite fitting that "Pictureessays" includes one. This work represents not only the fruits of a wonderful career by an experienced and caring character; it also symbolizes a skill that is fading with the advances of technology.

In a world where picture-taking has become instantaneous, the art of real photography has all but disappeared. With digital cameras that instantly display auto-focused, electronically exposed, full-color outcomes, the skills and patience of real photography are no longer so much in demand.

For more than a half century, Bill Ramsey clearly understood the technical side of photography. But more importantly, he had an eye for it. He knew a photo when he saw it and he had the patience, confidence, and skills to capture it.

But, beyond his photographic talents, Bill was truly a caring picture-taker.

So many of Bill's pictures are but simple snapshots of ordinary people standing next to others...some whom the world may have defined as celebrities. He understood that people would enjoy and appreciate someone capturing those moments on film.

Bill, who met a number of celebrities during his career, once told me that the most impressive person he ever met was Mother Teresa. During her brief visit to Omaha, Bill snapped countless photos of local folks with the wonderful woman from Calcutta. And, as he did so many times, Bill shared those photos with everyone involved.

For Bill Ramsey, taking pictures was not a skill, but a passion.

Being the good Catholic he is, when Bill's time on earth has ended, I won't be surprised to see him buried with a rosary in one hand and a camera in the other.

And as he enters heaven, Mother Teresa may be on hand to welcome a caring friend. But, Bill being Bill, he will look past her welcome and immediately ask her to stand next to St. Peter. Then he'll raise his old-fashioned 35mm camera to his eye and as he works to bring the shot into sharp focus the Saint and will-be-Saint will hear Bill say, "Ah, this is going to be a great picture!"

Tom Schmitt
Publisher, The Daily Nonpareil

"A friend"

Afterword

I am not afraid of tomorrow, for I have seen yesterday, and I love today.

— William Allen White

Photo: Jon Leu, The Daily Nonpareil

"You didn't write that book." Ms. Stowe paused a moment and then responded: "You are correct, sir. I didn't write this book; I held the pen and God moved my hand."

I suspect that most writers, upon reviewing what they have written, have that same experience — I could not possibly have written all those words with such feeling and meaning. The inspiration had to come from a higher power. I know that prayer is an integral part of writing and taking pictures.

My dream was to bring down the curtain on my aspiration to be an author with a pictorial history, and to stroll with you down memory lane. Thanks to the support and encouragement of family, friends and benefactors, the dream has come alive on the pages of this volume.

I hope that my love of America and her people is reflected in the words and images crafted for this work.

My closing thought: Work hard, be kind.

William E. Ramsey
Autumn 2010

I can't believe that we did the whole thing in seven months! It's called teamwork. We are elated, exhausted, and deeply grateful.

Other books have consumed from one year to more than four years to complete. I can honestly say that few things in life are more satisfying than writing a book. It is here today, tomorrow and well into the future. It's a legacy for family, friends, and strangers.

Which reminds me of the story of Harriet Beecher Stowe, author of "Uncle Tom's Cabin."

When she was on a lecture tour promoting her masterpiece, a strange thing happened. After her talk, a man shouted with disdain from the audience:

PICTURE essays

A journey through life with camera in hand

Bibliography

"Aksarben Village." In Wikipedia.org. Retrieved from http://en.wikipedia.org/wiki/Aksarben_Village (accessed 2010, June 13).

"Aksarben Village offers groundbreaking concepts." (2007, October 24 Omaha World-Herald.

Bicak, Carol. (2010, July 24). Take a visual voyage: South Omaha offers treats for the eyes. Omaha World-Herald.

"Bill Cosby." In Wikipedia.org. Retrieved from http://en.wikipedia.org/wiki/Bill_Cosby (accessed 2010, August 29).

"Blackstone Hotel (Omaha, Nebraska)." In Wikipedia.org. Retrieved from http://en.wikipedia.org/wiki/Blackstone_Hotel_(Omaha,_Nebraska) (accessed 2010, August 11).

"Boys Town (organization)." In Wikipedia.org. Retrieved from http://en.wikipedia.org/wiki/Boys_Town_(organization) (accessed 2010, August 14).

Bradley, James, with Powers, Rob. (2000). Flags of Our Fathers. New York: Bantam Books.

Burbach, Christopher. (2010, June 19). Rosenblatt memories endure in fans' hearts. Omaha World-Herald.

"Blair Buswell." In Wikipedia.org. Retrieved from http://en.wikipedia.org/wiki/Blair_Buswell (accessed 2010, September 12).

Carter, John E. (December 2008). Four Boys. The Banner: Douglas County Historical Society Newsletter.

"Catholic Radio on the Grow." (September 2010). Spirit Catholic Radio Network: KVSS Catholic Communications, Inc. Newsletter.

"Chapel/Visitor Center." Retrieved from http://holyfamilyshrineproject.com/index.php?option=com_content&view=article&id=39&Itemid=91 (accessed 2010, September 12).

"Cinema Treasures." Retrieved from http://cinematreasure.org/ (accessed 2010, September 4).

"Chip Davis." In Wikipedia.org. Retrieved from http://en.wikipedia.org/wiki/Chip_Davis (accessed 2010, September 30).

Chaney, Hunter. (2010, July 16). Wings of Freedom. Jewish Press.

"Charles W. Durham." Retrieved from http://stories.nufoundation.org/node/546 (accessed 2010, June 8).

"Coldstream Guards." In Wikipedia.org. Retrieved from http://en.wikipedia.org/wiki/Coldstream_Guards (accessed 2010, June 12).

"Creighton Orpheum Theater." In Wikipedia.org. Retrieved from http://en.wikipedia.org/wiki/Creighton_Orpheum_Theater (accessed 2010, September 4).

"Creighton Prep: Carmen & Don Leahy Stadium." Retrieved from http://creightonprep.creighton.edu/page.cfm?p=2301 (accessed 2010, September 16).

"Creighton Prep honors Don Leahy." (2010, September 3). Catholic Voice.

"Dick Cheney." In Wikipedia.org. Retrieved from http://en.wikipedia.org/wiki/Dick_Cheney (accessed 2010, July 4).

"Dingle Bay." In Wikipedia.org. Retrieved from http://en.wikipedia.org/wiki/Dingle_Bay (accessed 2010, July 26).

"DHHS Veterans' Homes Celebrate 120 Years!" Retrieved from http://www.hhs.state.ne.us/newsroom/newsreleases/2007/Oct/vetshome120.htm (accessed 2010, May 18).

"Don Leahy." Retrieved from http://www.omahasportshalloffame.com/dleahy-profile.php (accessed 2010, September 16).

"Douglas County." Retrieved from http://www.nacone.org/webpages/counties/countywebs/douglas.htm (accessed 2010, August 31).

"Douglas County Courthouse (Omaha, Nebraska)." In Wikipedia.org. Retrieved from http://en.wikipedia.org/wiki/Douglas_County_Courthouse_(Omaha,_Nebraska) (accessed 2010, July 26).

Durbin, Kristin. (2009, June 12). Stinson Park Unveiled for Summer Events. Midlands Business Journal.

"Dr. Lee Simmons." Retrieved from http://www.omaha.com/article/20091011/NEWS01/710119876 (accessed 2010, September 2).

"Edward J. Fraughton." In Wikipedia.org. Retrieved from http://en.wikipedia.org/wiki/Edward_fraughton (accessed 2010, September 12).

"Elmwood Tower (Omaha, Nebraska)." In Wikipedia.org. Retrieved from http://en.wikipedia.org/wiki/Masonic_Manor (accessed 2010, August 20).

"Eugene A. Leahy." Retrieved from http://www.omahapressclub.org/events/mayorleahy.htm (accessed 2010, June 2).

"Eugene A. Leahy." In Wikipedia.org. Retrieved from http://en.wikipedia.org/wiki/Eugene_A._Leahy (accessed 2010, July 12).

"Famous Racehorses." Retrieved from http://www.horsehats.com/famous-racehorses.html (accessed 2010, June 13).

"Fertile Ground in Omaha, Nebraska." Retrieved from http://www.heritagepreservation.org/RPM/FertileGround.html (accessed 2010, May 31).

"First National Center (Omaha)." In Wikipedia.org. Retrieved from http://en.wikipedia.org/wiki/First_National_Center_(Omaha) (accessed 2010, July 11).

"First National Sculpture Parks, First National Campus." Retrieved from http://www.firstnationalcampus.com/fnc/html/en/sculpture_park/default.html (accessed 2010, September 12).

"First Unitarian Church of Omaha." In Wikipedia.org. Retrieved from http://en.wikipedia.org/wiki/First_Unitarian_Church_of_Omaha (accessed 2010, May 11).

"Forest Lawn Cemetery." Retrieved from http://www.steveandmarta.com/graveyards/forest_lawn/forest_lawn_1.htm (accessed 2010, July 1).

"Forest Lawn Omaha History." Retrieved from http://www.forestlawnomaha.com/history.htm (accessed 2010, July 1).

"Fort Omaha." In Wikipedia.org. Retrieved from http://en.wikipedia.org/wiki/Fort_Omaha (accessed 2010, September 16).

"Fort Rosecrans National Cemetery." In Wikipedia.org. Retrieved from http://en.wikipedia.org/wiki/Fort_Rosecrans_National_Cemetery (accessed 2010, May 18).

"Franklin Delano Roosevelt Memorial (National Park Service)." Retrieved from http://www.nps.gov/fdrm/ (accessed 2010, July 4).

"Gary Lee Price." In Wikipedia.org. Retrieved from http://en.wikipedia.org/wiki/Gary_Lee_Price (accessed 2010, August 21).

"Gene Leahy Mall." In Wikipedia.org. Retrieved from http://en.wikipedia.org/wiki/Gene_Leahy_Mall (accessed 2010, July 12).

"General Cook House Museum." Retrieved from http://www.omahahistory.org/museum.htm (accessed 2010, September 16).

Gerber, Kristine, and Spencer, Jeffrey S. (2003). Building For The Ages: Omaha's Architectural Landmarks. Omaha, NE: Landmarks, Inc.

"Gordon MacRae." In Wikipedia.org. Retrieved from http://en.wikipedia.org/wiki/Gordon_MacRae (accessed 2010, September 11).

"Grand Canyon." In Wikipedia.org. Retrieved from http://en.wikipedia.org/wiki/Grand_Canyon (accessed 2010, September 14).

"Grand Teton." In Wikipedia.org. Retrieved from http://en.wikipedia.org/wiki/Grand_Teton (accessed 2010, May 27).

Hansen, Matthew. (2010, July 14). Schlegel leaving a lasting mark. Omaha World-Herald.

Hendee, David. (2010, June 13). Saddle up for 150th anniversary of Pony Express. Omaha World-Herald.

Hendee, David. (2010, May 31). Willing to die for each other: Omaha's 'Babe' Gomez was still in his teens when he sacrificed his life for his fellow Marines. Omaha World-Herald.

"Henry Doorly Zoo." In Wikipedia.org. Retrieved from http://en.wikipedia.org/wiki/Henry_Doorly_Zoo (accessed 2010, June 29).

"Historic Prospect Hill — Omaha's Pioneer Cemetery." Retrieved from http://www.nebraskahistory.org/publish/markers/texts/prospect_hill_cemetery.htm (accessed 2010, June 26).

"History." Retrieved from http://www.ops.org/elementary/skinner/ABOUTOURSCHOOL/History/tabid/59/Default.aspx (accessed 2010, September 16).

"Holland Performing Arts Center." In Wikipedia.org. Retrieved from http://en.wikipedia.org/wiki/Holland_Performing_Arts_Center (accessed 2010, October 1).

"Holy Angels Church: History." Retrieved form http://www.holyangels.com/holyhist.htm (accessed 2010, June 20).

Horan, Judy. (2003). Some Kind of Hero. Mature Living, July/August 2003, 35-37.

"Hotel Fontenelle." In Wikipedia.org. Retrieved from http://en.wikipedia.org/wiki/Hotel_Fontenelle (accessed 2010, May 12).

"In Memory of John Mulhall." Retrieved from http://www.ogma.org/mulhall.html (accessed 2010, August 11).

"IMGP3040c." Retrieved from http://www.flickr.com/photos/presbyteer/84142011/in/set-1796758 (accessed 2010, June 2).

"Iowa School for the Deaf." Retrieved from http://www.iadeaf.k12.ia.us/isdabout/isdhistory.php (accessed 2010, August 21).

"Iowa School for the Deaf." In Wikipedia.org. Retrieved from http://en.wikipedia.org/wiki/Iowa_School_for_the_Deaf (accessed 2010, August 21).

"James Horan." Retrieved from http://www.asaa-avart.org/artists/biography.php?mem1d=54 (accessed 2010, June 6).

"J. L. Brandeis and Sons Store Building." In Wikipedia.org. Retrieved from http://en.wikipedia.org/wiki/J._L._Brandeis_and_Sons_Store_Building (accessed 2010, August 31).

"Johnny Parle, Who Didn't Hesitate to Die, Is Home at Last." (1943, May 29). Omaha World-Herald.

"Johnny Rosenblatt Stadium." In Wikipedia.org. Retrieved from http://en.wikipedia.org/wiki/Johnny_Rosenblatt_Stadium (accessed 2010, August 31).

Jordan, Steve. (2009, September 25). Salute set for Richard Holland. Omaha World-Herald.

"Joslyn Art Museum." In Wikipedia.org. Retrieved from http://en.wikipedia.org/wiki/Joslyn_Art_Museum (accessed 2010, May 18).

"Joslyn Castle." In Wikipedia.org. Retrieved from http://en.wikipedia.org/wiki/Joslyn_Castle (accessed 2010, May 31).

"Kay A. Orr." In Wikipedia.org. Retrieved from http://en.wikipedia.org/wiki/Kay_A._Orr (accessed 2010, August 25).

Kelly, Michael. (2010, June 5). Her 'Turn around' changed many lives. Omaha World-Herald.

Kelly, Michael. (2010, June 19). Legacy of Rosenblatt more than a stadium. Omaha World-Herald.

Kelly, Michael. (2010, June 12). Shower of cash and a mystery. Omaha World-Herald.

Kelly, Michael. (2010, June 24). Stadium generates sense of family pride. Omaha World-Herald.

"Kiewit Corporation." In Wikipedia.org. Retrieved from http://en.wikipedia.org/wiki/Kiewit_Corporation (accessed 2010, June 29).

Klinker, Adam, Kaufman, Kirby, and Pandil-Eaton, Whitney. (2010, September 12). Rescuers' Sacrifices Saluted. Omaha World-Herald.

Lavigne, Paula. Omaha artist says fans make CWS. Retrieved from http://sports.espn.go.com/ncaa/news/story?id=5289472

"List of bridges on the National Register of Historic Places in Iowa." In Wikipedia.org. Retrieved from http://en.wikipedia.org/wiki/List_of_bridges_on_the_National_Register_of_Historic_Places_in_Iowa (accessed 2010, June 16).

"Livestock Exchange Building (Omaha, Nebraska)." In Wikipedia.org. Retrieved from http://en.wikipedia.org/wiki/Livestock_Exchange_Building_(Omaha,_Nebraska).

"Lou Holtz." In Wikipedia.org. Retrieved from http://en.wikipedia.org/wiki/Lou_Holtz (accessed 2010, May 15).

"Madison County, Iowa." In Wikipedia.org. Retrieved from http://en.wikipedia.org/wiki/Madison_County,_Iowa (accessed 2010, June 14).

"Maria von Trapp." In Wikipedia.org. Retrieved from http://en.wikipedia.org/wiki/Maria_von_Trapp (accessed 2010, July 11).

"Maya Angelou." Retrieved from http://mayaangelou.com/ (accessed 2010, May 11).

"Mayor of Omaha   Omaha Commons." Retrieved from http://omaha.ne.us.towncommons.com/Mayor_of_Omaha (accessed 2010, June 18).

McGrath, Jim, editor and compiler. (2001). HEARTBEAT: George Bush in His Own Words. New York: Scribner.

"Memorial Park (Omaha)." In Wikipedia.org. Retrieved from http://en.wikipedia.org/wiki/Memorial_Park_(Omaha) (accessed 2010, July 4).

"Menorah (Hanukkah)." In Wikipedia.org. Retrieved from http://en.wikipedia.org/wiki/Menorah_(Hanukkah) (accessed 2010, July 18).

"Midtown Omaha." In Wikipedia.org. Retrieved from http://en.wikipedia.org/wiki/Midtown_Omaha (accessed 2010, July 26).

Mihelich, Dennis N. (2006). The History of Creighton University 1878-2003. Omaha: Creighton University Press.

"Morrison Stadium." In Wikipedia.org. Retrieved from http://en.wikipedia.org/wiki/Morrison_Stadium (accessed 2010, September 4).

"Motor Torpedo Boat PT-109." In Wikipedia.org. Retrieved from http://en.wikipedia.org/wiki/Motor_Torpedo_Boat_PT-109 (accessed 2010, August 11).

"Movies and Live Bands at Stinson Park at Aksarben Village in Omaha NE." Retrieved from http://activerain.com/blogsview/1185125/movies-and-live-bands-at-stinson-park-at-aksarben-village-in-Omaha-NE (accessed 2010, August 27).

"NCCJ Honors Kiewit as 'Brotherhood Builder.'" (1967, October 4). Omaha World-Herald.

"NEBRASKAland Foundation Awards." Retrieved from http://www.nebraskalandfoundation.org//awards.php (accessed 2010, May 21).

"Norfolk Veterans' Home." Retrieved from http://www.hhs.state.ne.us/newsroom/press_kits/120_Year_Vets_Celebration/NVH/ (accessed 2010, May 11).

"Old City Hall (Omaha)." In Wikipedia.org. Retrieved from http://en.wikipedia.org/wiki/Old_City_Hall_(Omaha) (accessed 2010, May 11).

"Offutt Air Force Base." In Wikipedia.org. Retrieved from http://en.wikipedia.org/wiki/Offutt_Air_Force_Base (accessed 2010, August 14).

"Omaha Central High School." In Wikipedia.org. Retrieved from http://en.wikipedia.org/wiki/Omaha_Central_High_School (accessed 2010, August 30).

"Omaha Firefighters' Memorial." Retrieved from http://omahafirefighters-memorial.com/ (accessed 2010, September 11).

"Omaha Landmarks." In Wikipedia.org. Retrieved from http://en.wikipedia.org/wiki/Omaha_landmarks (accessed 2010, May 18).

"Omaha Performing Arts." Retrieved from http://www.omahaperformingarts.org/orpheum/history/default.aspx (accessed 2010, September 4).

"Omaha Police Memorial." Retrieved from http://www.publicartomaha.org/art/info/92/Omaha%20Police%20Memorial (accessed 2010, September 13).

"Omaha sculptor Matthew Placzek commissioned to realize John David Brcin's bronze sculpture 'Sioux Warrior.'" Retrieved from http://www.tfaoi.com/aa/8aa/8aa188.htm (accessed 2010, June 5).

"One First National Center, Omaha, U.S.A." Retrieved from http://www.emporis.com/application/?nav=building&lng=3&id=101138 (accessed 2010, July 11).

"Packer's National Bank Building." In Wikipedia.org. Retrieved from http://en.wikipedia.org/wiki/Packer%27s_National_Bank_Building (accessed 2010, September 15).

"Peony Park." In Wikipedia.org. Retrieved from http://en.wikipedia.org/wiki/Peony_Park (accessed 2010, August 20).

"Pioneer Courage Park, First National Campus." http://www.firstnational-campus.com/fnc/html/en/sculpture_park/pioneer.html (accessed 2010, September 12).

"Prospect Hill Cemetery (North Omaha, Nebraska)." In Wikipedia.org. Retrieved from http://en.wikipedia.org/wiki/Prospect_Hill_Cemetery_(North_Omaha,_Nebraska) (accessed 2010, June 26).

"Public Private Partnerships-Village within the City." Retrieved from http://www.villageprofile.com/nebraska/omaha/03/topic.html (accessed 2010, June 14).

Ramsey, William E. (1980, January 27). Omaha Has Been Good To the Immigrant Boy. Sunday World-Herald Magazine of the Midlands.

Ramsey, William E. (January 1959). The Story of Gwinnie Kay. Franciscan Message.

Ramsey, William E. (Summer 1994). Senator Robert Kennedy spoke at Creighton University. BRiefs.

Reinecke, Sarah. (2010, July 17). Flights of history: Planes that helped win World War II visit Omaha. Omaha World-Herald.

"Richard Cushing." In Wikipedia.org. Retrieved from http://en.wikipedia. org/wiki/Richard_Cushing (accessed 2010, August 2).

"Roger Welsch." In Wikipedia.org. Retrieved from http://en.wikipedia.org/ wiki/Roger_Welsch (accessed 2010, August 20).

Rohwer, Tim. (2010, July 21). Main Street mania: Growing support for downtown revitalization. The Daily Nonpareil.

"Schlegel Retirement: Creighton achievements." (2010, July 15). Omaha World-Herald.

"Seldin and Stoney: 2010 Omaha Business Hall of Fame Inductees." Retrieved from http://www.omahachamber.org/News/newsdetail. aspx?StoryID=15317 (accessed 2010, July 22).

"Sidey Returns To C.B." (2002, November 20). The Daily Nonpareil.

"Some Choice!" Northern Natural News. May 1964.

"Speed Graphic." In Wikipedia.org. Retrieved from http://en.wikipedia. org/wiki/Speed_Graphic (accessed 2010, June 18).

"St. Cecilia Cathedral." In Wikipedia.org. Retrieved from http:// en.wikipedia.org/wiki/St._Cecilia_Cathedral (accessed 2010, June 27).

"Stephen Ambrose." In Wikipedia.org. Retrieved from http://en.wikipedia. org/wiki/Stephen_Ambrose (accessed 2010, September 25).

"St. Peter's Square — Statue of St. Peter." http://saintpetersbasilica.org/Exterior/StPeterStatue/StPeterStatue.htm (accessed 2010, August 3).

"Strategic Air and Space Museum." Retrieved from http://www.sasmuseum.com/about-us/ (accessed 2010, July 4).

"Swiss Guard." In Wikipedia.org. Retrieved from http://en.wikipedia.org/ wiki/Swiss_Guard (accessed 2010, August 3).

"TD Ameritrade Park Omaha." In Wikipedia.org. Retrieved from http:// en.wikipedia.org/wiki/TD_Ameritrade_Park_Omaha (accessed 2010, June 5).

"Ted Kooser." In Wikipedia.org. Retrieved from http://en.wikipedia.org/ wiki/Ted_Kooser (accessed 2010, June 24).

"The Bridges of Madison County." In Wikipedia.org. Retrieved from http://en.wikipedia.org/wiki/The_Bridges_of_Madison_County (accessed 2010, June 12).

"The Capping of the Washington Monument." Retrieved from http://www. theroadtoemmaus.org/RdLb/21PbAr/Hst/US/WashMonCap.htm (accessed 2010, April 24).

"The Cliffs of Moher." In cliffs-moher.com. Retrieved from http:///.cliffs-moher.com/about.php (accessed 2010, May 11).

"The Mission and Story." Retrieved from http://holyfamilyshrineproject. com/index.php?option=com_content&view=article&id=40&Item id=92 (accessed 2010, September 12).

The New Jerusalem Bible: Reader's Edition. New York: Doubleday, 1989.

"The Salvation Army." Retrieved from http://chattanooga.careerlink.com/ employer/profile/324 (accessed 2010, August 20)

"Thomas S. Ricketts" In Wikipedia.org. Retrieved from http:// en.wikipedia.org/wiki/Thomas_S._Ricketts (accessed 2010, October 2).

"Trinity Cathedral (Omaha, Nebraska)." In Wikipedia.org. Retrieved from http://en.wikipedia.org/wiki/Trinity_Cathedral_(Omaha,_Nebraska) (accessed 2010, May 12).

"United Effort Earned the Brotherhood Award." (1967, October 8). Omaha World-Herald.

United States Department of the Interior National Park Service. National Register of Historic Places Continuation Sheet. Section 8, p. 6.

"United Way of the Midlands ¬¬ Mission and Vision." Retrieved from http://www.uwmidlands.org/mission-and-vision.html (accessed 2010, May 12).

"USS Hazard (AM-240)." In Wikipedia.org. Retrieved from http:// en.wikipedia.org/wiki/USS_Hazard_(AM-240) (accessed 2010, September 21).

"USS Hornet (CV-12)." In Wikipedia.org. Retrieved from http:// en.wikipedia.org/wiki/USS_Hornet_(CV-12) (accessed 2010, September 15).

"Vice President Spiro Agnew." Retrieved from http://www.omahapress-club.org/events/SpiroAgnew.htm (accessed 2010, June 3).

"Washington Monument." In Wikipedia.org. Retrieved from http:// en.wikipedia.org/wiki/Washington_Monument (accessed 2010, April 24).

"Welcome to the Omaha Press Club." Retrieved from http://www.omahap-ressclub.org/events/BettyAbbott.htm (accessed 2010, July 11).

"Welcome to Sarpy County." Retrieved from http://www.gosarpy.com/at-tractions/points.asp (accessed 2010, September 12).

"Winter Park Colorado Summer Vacation." Retrieved from http://www. buzzle.com/articles/winter-park-colorado-summer-vacation (accessed 2010, August 30).

"Woodmen of the World." In Wikipedia.org. Retrieved from http:// en.wikipedia.org/wiki/Woodmen_of_the_World (accessed 2010, May 11).

Zimmer, Ed. (2009). Wyuka Cemetery: A Driving & Walking Tour. Lincoln, Nebraska: Eagle Printing Company.

"Zorinsky Lake Park in Omaha, Nebraska." Retrieved from http://road7. blogspot.com/2008/11/zorinsky-lake-park-in-omaha-nebraska.html (accessed 2010, June 18).

Zuegner, Chuck and Ramsey, William E., editors. (October 1971). May We Present...The Beautiful Omaha Press Club." Beyond-30-: The Local Monthly Omaha Press Club Newsletter.

Index